Days

to a More
Powerful Vocabulary

Also by The Princeton Language Institute

21st Century Dictionary of Quotations
21st Century Grammar Handbook
Roget's 21st Century Thesaurus

10
Days
to a More Powerful Vocabulary

The Princeton Language Institute
and Tom Nash, Ph.D.

Produced by The Philip Lief Group, Inc.

WARNER BOOKS

A Time Warner Company

Copyright © 2001 by The Philip Lief Group Inc.
All rights reserved.
Produced by The Philip Lief Group, Inc.

Warner Books, Inc., 1271 Avenue of the Americas, New York, NY 10020

Visit our Web site at www.twbookmark.com

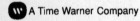 A Time Warner Company

Printed in the United States of America

First Printing: July 2001

10   9   8   7   6   5   4   3   2   1

Library of Congress Cataloging-in-Publication Data
10 days to a more powerful vocabulary / the Princeton Language Institute.
        p. cm.
      ISBN 0-446-67669-1
      1. Vocabulary—Problems, exercises, etc. I. Title: Ten days to a more powerful vocabulary. II. Princeton Language Institute.

PE1449 .A13 2001
428.1—dc21   00-043835

Book design by Ralph Fowler
Cover design by Jon Valk

This book is dedicated to my uncle and aunt, Paul and Pauline Edquist, who showered me with love and kindness—and to Karol, whose mind and heart I admire.

Acknowledgments

I wish to thank several people. Foremost is Nancy Salucci, who contributed immensely to this book in her dual role as researcher and editorial assistant. Other important suggestions came from writer Diane Hall of Jacksonville, Oregon, who was especially helpful with medical terminology. My son, Paul Nash, furnished valuable insights on the language of musical performance. Eileen Koutnik and Jamie Saxon of The Philip Lief Group provided a good critical eye and helpful suggestions. Thanks to all.

Contents

Introduction

Not long ago, I found a *Doonesbury* cartoon featuring a brief conversation between two clueless Walden freshmen. In the six panels, writer Garry Trudeau dropped the words *fractious, Balkanized, plurality, feckless,* and *penal.* Like many other readers, I'm sure, I went looking for my dictionary.

What's going on here? We're not talking about the editorial page or the foreign affairs section of the paper. On this particular Sunday, *Doonesbury* was wedged into a slot between *Beetle Bailey* and *Peanuts,* two cartoons that make *Dick and Jane* look like *War and Peace.* How can a popular artist like Trudeau ask so much of his readers without losing his audience? The answer is simple. We want to know more about language, the single element that best defines our humanity. We like the challenge of learning new words. And even the comics inform us.

Words fascinate us. We buy dictionaries and word games. We labor over crosswords and anagrams. We watch shows such as *Jeopardy!* ("Foreign Words for $100, Alex") with a plethora of language categories. Even the people who make us laugh—Stephen Wright, David Letterman, George Carlin—regularly play with words, asking questions like "Why do they call it *stop-and-go* traffic? Shouldn't it be *go-and-stop* traffic?" or "Why do they call it *quicksand* if it sucks you down slowly?" Good questions.

Language is not just a fascination, however. Words also define us. We are awash in a sea of wonderful words and

reach out to grasp so few. Yet, successful people and the people we most respect are often wordsmiths, capable of turning
phrases to great advantage—these people depend on a rich
word bank to inspire action, achieve economic goals, and up-
lift the human spirit. The keys to success are many, but few
are more important than being able to speak and write with
clarity and precision.

Increasing your vocabulary is an act of self-improvement,
not unlike getting physically fit or putting your finances in
order. As with working out, you need to follow a systematic
plan. Manic lifting of barbells on Day One leads to Ben-Gay
rubdowns on Day Two, not body fitness. Similarly, a random
word search from this day forward would probably create
more frustration than vocabulary growth. So, *10 Days to a
More Powerful Vocabulary* offers an incremental, measured
journey toward word-building success. Through the course
of your ten-day journey, you will learn key terms from categories such as medicine, science, government, music, and
history. Along the way, you will be asked to test your knowledge with quizzes and exercises. Don't worry! You'll have fun!
Furthermore, you will learn new ways to seek out and then
practice vocabulary words in everyday settings from e-mail to
business gatherings. Grab a pencil and scribble your homework right in the pages of the book. In less than a week and a
half, you should see some real progress toward your speaking
and writing goals.

I like to say that vocabulary lists are like keys. The world is
full of doors and passageways, each leading to a richer life. To
unlock these doors—economic portals, social barriers, personal gateways—you need the right keys. Open the pages,
take the first steps, start gathering keys. I think you will
enjoy the ten-day journey.

10
Days

to a More
Powerful Vocabulary

Day 1

Getting Started

The Power of a Great Vocabulary

Words carry more influence and importance than we think. How we express ourselves means far more than the clothes we wear or the cars we drive. People with strong vocabularies can rivet others' attention with the turn of a phrase; they can converse easier, always seeming to know "just the right thing to say" on any occasion; they can express their ideas with more creativity and color; they are more eloquent and powerful writers and communicators; and they are more effective in the workplace. Wordsmithing is a skill that people admire.

The good news is that increasing your vocabulary is easy and fun. You can start at any age. Newspaper crossword puzzles, board games like Scrabble, and even game shows like *Jeopardy!* attest to our national fascination with words. Keeping word lists and using new words should become part of your daily routine. In the morning as you head for work, in the evening as you unwind—anytime when you have a moment for yourself—add a word or two to your lists. If you add just three words a day, by this time next year you'll be richer by almost 1,100 words. So let's spend ten days expanding your word bank, or word database.

Calculate Your Word Bank

A good place to start is to look at your working vocabulary as it is now. Here's a practical and accurate way to compute your *lexicon* (vocabulary).

1. Pick four pages in a standard dictionary at random—for example, pages 100, 145, 210, and 237. Count the total number of entries on these pages.

2. How many of these words do you recognize? For example, how many of these words have you come across in your reading or heard at work or a social gathering? Get out your calculator. Take the number of words you are familiar with and divide by the total number of words on the four pages.

3. What percentage of the total words on the four pages do you know?

   • If you recognize 80 percent or more of the words, you are brilliant. Your vocabulary is superior.

   • If you recognize 70 percent of the words, you have a strong command of the English language. Your vocabulary is impressive.

   • If you recognize 60 percent, you are well spoken and most likely possess excellent writing skills. Congratulations.

   • If you recognize 50 percent of the entries, you have an above-average vocabulary.

- If you recognize 40 percent, there's room for improvement, but you have a good base.

- If you recognize 30 percent of the words, you probably wandered into the Z's. *Nobody* knows words like *zygote, zymogenesis,* and *zygapophysis.*

- If you recognize less than 30 percent, you found your old French book from high school. That's a *faux pas* (mistake).

Key Terms: Tools for Opening Doors

Let's begin with the notion of words as keys. Imagine a long hallway passing a number of rooms. Inside each room is a conversation, a party, a performance, a financial deal—something exciting, appealing, valuable. Many of the doors are open, but others are locked. The doors might be marked "Computers" or "Government" or "Science and Math." To gain entry, you need to know the meaning of particular nouns, verbs, and adjectives—the cultural and commercial passwords of those inside. In organizing these word lists, you are looking for the *shibboleths* of each interest group—that is, the key terms that people in each arena use among their peers. How do you readers join the fun? Through language.

Key Terms to Enter Cyberspace

There's no better place to start looking at new words than the Internet. In a 1999 article for a *New York Times* e-commerce issue, Pam Belluck writes that within the next decade, those who are "wired" will enjoy more opportunities, higher incomes, and richer lives. Those who are not computer literate will be like residents of Los Angeles who don't own cars. Even in the few short years since the Internet, many new terms have emerged.

- **http:** HyperText Transport Protocol, the scheme used to carry Web pages over the Internet.

- **URL:** Uniform Resource Locator, commonly referred to as a Web address, for example, http://www.iecc.com.

- **Domain:** A particular location on an Internet address. For example, bigwords.com can be found at the address www.bigwords.com.

- **HTML:** HyperText Markup Language, the set of codes used in Web pages to indicate headings, links to other pages, font changes, and the like.

- **Portals:** The term refers to high-visibility Web sites that promise to guide you on your search. Yahoo! is one such portal.

- **Virtual:** This term refers to things that exist *only* with the help of computers. For example, virtual reality video games must be played on a computer; they create a realistic world, but only with the help of computers.

- **Cyberspace** (coined by novelist William Gibson): Cyberspace is the imaginary place where Internet things happen, as in "I met my wife in cyberspace at www.lonelyhearts.com."

- **Interactive:** Means a two-way transaction online. An interactive site might encourage sampling or testing of a product.

- **Byte:** The unit in which computer storage is measured. One byte can store one character. The word *indefeasible* takes 12 bytes. (By the way, *indefeasible* means "not capable of being annulled or undone.")

- **RAM:** The term stands for Random Access Memory, the primary memory that a computer uses while it's running.

- **ROM:** The term stands for Read Only Memory, which has fixed contents set at the factory. Most computers contain a small ROM with the program that starts the computer when you turn it on.

- **README:** The conventional name for a file provided as part of a software package with introductory information. Usually spelled README or README.TXT.

- **DVD:** Digital Video Disc or Digital Versatile Disc, the new version of a CD, which can store far more information. Used for both recorded movies and software.

- **Gopher:** A system of menus for accessing the Internet that has not completely disappeared.

- **Telnet:** A system for connecting to computers over a network and using the computer as though you're sitting at its console. Only computer geeks use it.

Top Ten List: The Best Ways to Increase Your Vocabulary

1. **Subscribe to an Internet vocabulary service such as Wordsmith.** At www.wordsmith.org, you can receive a word a day (AWAD) without charge. The words automatically appear on your e-mail each morning, and it is possible to download archives of past words as well.

2. **Try difficult crossword puzzles regularly.** The *New York Times* puzzle is among the most challenging, but also the most rewarding for acquiring and practicing new words. To really challenge yourself, do the acrostic puzzle as well. When you start doing either in pen, you know you're a vocabulary ace! If you prefer to work on the Net, try Online Crosswords. Type in the keywords *online + crosswords*, and you'll be connected to more than 3,600 sites, including Star Wars Crosswords, Bible Crosswords, Kids' Crosswords, Sports Crosswords, TV Crosswords, and puzzles from major daily newspapers all over the world.

3. **Go to a bookstore or used bookstore, and buy as many Charles Dickens novels as you can find.** Dickens writes about everything—from business to education—and his vocabulary, always fascinating, is still relevant today. Dickens, who wrote serialized novels that appeared in magazines, had a strong sense of audience. His vocabulary reflected that of Londoners on the rise—people who were looking to use language as a step to a better life. Dickens is instructive even today. May I suggest *The Pickwick Papers*?

4. **Play word games.** Put Scrabble, Balderdash, Perquacky, and Word Yahtzee on your holiday wish list. Do not cheat unless you're playing an overachieving teenager who needs to be taken down a notch.

5. **Subscribe to magazines.** Go ahead and keep your subscription to the *National Enquirer* if you must. But you will be amazed at how you can increase your vocabulary by digesting articles from worthies like *Discovery* magazine, *The Atlantic Monthly, The New*

Yorker, Scientific American, or *Omni.* You will learn neat stuff, too.

6. **Buy a book with a glossary of Latin and Greek roots (usually in the back).** Look first in a used bookstore. Knowledge of a small number of Latin and Greek forms (chron-, log-, phon-) can unlock the meanings of thousands of important English words.

7. **Surf the Net.** Devote a half hour a day—or whatever you can spare—browsing cyberspace. Get on your browser and simply type in a key word of something that interests you (*dinosaurs, truffles, Monet*) and follow the trail. University Web sites are terrific places to visit, but they're not your only good resources. Building a vocabulary is largely a matter of reading new words in context.

8. **Listen to tapes in the car.** Tired of listening to mindless blather and commercials during your commute? Borrow a tape recorder with a microphone attachment (you can often check out audio equipment from your local library), then make a vocabulary tape with words from this book and others that you glean from your own reading and listening. Play the tape on your car's sound system.

9. **Use it or lose it.** Practice new words. Use them in letters, memos, e-mails, and conversations. Try not to sound like a thesaurus, but sneak an occasional *quixotic* (romantically impractical) or *uxorious* (submissive to one's wife) into the daily grind. It will be fun.

10. **Watch public television and listen to National Public Radio.** Television programs like *Charlie Rose, The BBC World News,* documentaries, and even animal and wildlife shows, and radio programs like *All Things*

Considered and *Fresh Air* expose you to a new world of words, easy to learn since they're presented in the context of a conversation (like an interview) or a story. Take advantage. Believe me, reruns of sitcoms don't cut it.

Lessons from Mom: Do Your Homework Before You Watch TV

Perhaps you remember this one. I do. As I settled into the big overstuffed couch for an evening of *The Jeffersons, Star Trek,* or *The Partridge Family,* Mom made it clear that work comes before play. "Do your homework before you watch TV" was the evening prompt that led to hours of long division, German word lists, and mapmaking. By the time those odious projects were tucked safely away, there wasn't much time left for *Rawhide* or *M*A*S*H.* But at least I was ready with an essay on *The Red Badge of Courage* for Miss Brooks's English class the following afternoon.

"Do your homework first" also applies to vocabulary building. At this point, you may be asking—and rightly so— what homework? Bad news. In life, there is always homework. Good news—you can make it fun. Let's trot down to the video store and pick up a double stack of movies. And while you're preparing for a night with Arnold Schwarzenegger, Meryl Streep, and Humphrey Bogart, use the resources at Video Warehouse to *augment* (enlarge, enhance) your word bank.

Movies for homework? Things could be worse. Okay, there are thousands of films here, many with challenging vocabulary words in the titles. Let's see what puzzlers you can find. Remember, you're just browsing the aisles here, not looking for *Gone With the Wind*.

Words and Movie Titles for $500

Now it's time to play your own version of *Jeopardy!* See if you can figure out the meaning of the following words.

1. *Apocalypse Now* (1979), starring Marlon Brando
2. *Chameleon* (1998), starring Bobbie Phillips
3. *The Matrix* (1999), starring Keanu Reeves
4. *Protocol* (1984), starring Goldie Hawn
5. *Monolith* (1994), starring Louis Gossett, Jr.
6. *Nemesis* (1993), starring Olivier Gruner

a. customs, formalities, conventions
b. pillar, column, monument
c. prophesied conclusion, holocaust
d. an animal who changes color depending on its environment
e. fate, fortune, unbeatable foe
f. grid, array, format (math)

ANSWERS: 1. c, 2. d, 3. f, 4. a, 5. b, 6. e

Words and Movie Titles for $1,000

Now you're ready for the next set. You just might encounter this set of words and movie titles in your next visit to the video store.

1. *Virtuosity* (1995), starring Denzel Washington
2. *Hybrid* (1997), starring John Barrymore III
3. *The Abomination* (1988), starring Scott Davis

a. excellence, often in performance
b. haunting, dark, mysterious
c. infamous, widely known

4. *Gothic* (1986),
   starring Gabriel Byrne

   d. horrible thing, repulsive
   object

5. *The Odyssey* (1997),
   starring Armand Assante

   e. crossbreed, elite mixture

6. *Notorious* (1946),
   starring Cary Grant

   f. a long and event-filled
   journey

ANSWERS: 1. a, 2. e, 3. d, 4. b, 5. f, 6. c

Very good. Now remember, whenever you wander down to the corner video store, you can also do as Mom says. Before slumping down with a big bag of popcorn and soda, put your word-sleuthing powers to work. Bring home *The Accidental Tourist* or *On the Waterfront,* but also jot down a dozen new vocabulary words while you're in the store. Either figure out their meanings from the jacket blurbs or look them up later.

Key Terms That "Give You the Business"

If you're preparing for an interview, applying for a job in the corporate world, or planning a client presentation, it's a good idea to brush up on your knowledge of business terms. Carefully using these terms in a conversation or letter can definitely impress. Practice these terms and make it a habit to read the business section of your newspaper to find other useful phrases and words.

- **cabal** (conspiracy, insider group, plotters): *The birthday party <u>cabal</u> managed to keep the surprise party a secret from the guest of honor by making the arrangements during her lunch hour.*

- **conglomerate** (a business group composed of companies from one or several industries): *Mary Ann* *decided to write her business school paper on a new* <u>conglomerate</u> *called the Phoenix Group, a group of companies with the objective of promoting economic growth in low-income areas of Arizona.*

- **entrepreneur** (person who starts a business or creates new kinds of businesses): *In the twenty-first century, key tasks of an* <u>entrepreneur</u> *include financing new business technology and exploring online applications to stay ahead of the competition.*

- **extrapolate** (estimate or predict based on trends): *Frank, head of the marketing division, added up current income figures and* <u>extrapolated</u> *into the year 2005, predicting a sales level of $3.2 million.*

- **fraudulent** (deceitful, false, crooked): *Margaret filed a* <u>fraudulent</u> *expense report after she returned from a business trip with a new wardrobe.*

- **infrastructure** (foundation, basic underlying structure): *Once our consultant had completed two weeks of training and hiring within our marketing division, we felt confident we had the necessary* <u>infrastructure</u> *to handle all the requests for added services from overseas clients.*

- **jurisdiction** (ownership, legal control over a particular area): *The sales team in Los Angeles wanted to hold a special event to promote their product line in Oakland, but that city was out of their* <u>jurisdiction</u>. *It belonged to the Northern California sales team.*

- **liquidity** (availability of funds): *Marsha decided* <u>liquidity</u> *was her best financial strategy, so she sold her stocks.*

- **lucrative** (profitable): *The Timmons deal, one reflecting the company's new interest in high-tech medicine, proved* very _lucrative_, resulting in 20 percent higher profits than last year.

- **monopoly** (exclusive ownership or control): _New Internet companies are constantly fighting for a niche in cyberspace, but in many cases, the first e-commerce site in any given area, such as selling books online, already has a monopoly on sales._

- **paradigm** (a model, a pattern, a principle of organization): _If the dominant business paradigm in the twenty-first century is electronic commerce, also know as e-commerce, then every business should establish a presence on the Internet._

- **persona** ("mask," an adopted role): _For his keynote address at the meeting with the Shake the Pounds corporation, Jack adopted the persona of Richard Simmons._

Pop Quiz: Business Terms

All right. It's time to see if you can match the key business term with the correct definition. For this exercise, adopt your best test-taking _persona_.

1. jurisdiction	a. estimate	
2. extrapolate	b. a mask	
3. monopoly	c. model, pattern, principle of organization	
4. fraudulent	d. foundation, basic underlying structure	
5. paradigm	e. available funds	
6. liquidity	f. exclusive ownership or control	
7. cabal	g. ownership, dominion, legal control	

8. infrastructure   h. conspiracy, insider group
9. persona   i. deceitful, false, crooked
10. conglomerate   j. collection
11. lucrative   k. starter of a business
12. entrepreneur   l. profitable

ANSWERS: 1. g, 2. a, 3. f, 4. i, 5. c, 6. e, 7. h, 8. d, 9. b, 10. j, 11. l, 12. k

Some Extra Credit Business Words

- Remember Tom Cruise as Charlie Babbitt, the self-centered car salesman in the movie *Rain Man*? Cruise's character name comes from *Babbitt,* a 1922 novel by Sinclair Lewis. Someone who embraces questionable values, especially in business, engages in Babbitry, a kind of moral self-deception. Do you know any Charlie Babbitts?

- Is anyone in your business circle a *Luddite*? People who refuse to use modern technology like computers and voice mail are Luddites, named after Ned Ludd, who inspired the Luddite movement in England (1811–16), a series of mob attacks on new machinery and innovative factories. If the guy in the next cubicle clacks away on an electric typewriter, he may be a Luddite.

- A *pettifogger* is unscrupulous and devious, often a lawyer. In *The Simpsons,* Lionel Hutz is a *pettifogging* Springfield attorney. Fans of the bumbling, underhanded Hutz can find his whole sorry story at www.pettifogger.com/hutz.htm. Check it out.

- The office tyrant, one who specializes in backstabbing and self-promotion, is properly called *Machiavellian* (mak-ee-uh-VEL-ee-un). This word derives from the

Italian Renaissance bureaucrat Nicolo Machiavelli, best known for his work entitled *The Prince*.

Celebrity Word Association

Do you recall <u>E</u>very <u>G</u>ood <u>B</u>oy <u>D</u>oes <u>F</u>ine, the key words to remembering notes in the musical scale? Such clues are called *mnemonic* (nee-MON-ik) devices, meaning "memory-assisting strategies." As word sleuths, you can build your vocabulary by using word associations to create your own mnemonic devices.

What better way to make sound and spelling links than to associate words with famous people? So, here are some models for the game of Celebrity Word Association. When you're through with this list, try creating your own mnemonic devices.

- **algorithm** (repetitive, often mind-numbingly boring, problem-solving procedure, especially apt for computers): *When **Al Gore** gives a speech, it sounds like a computer grinding out an **algorithm** to locate the secret code for a bank vault.*

- **recalcitrant** (rebellious, stubborn): ***Cal Ripken** of the Baltimore Orioles was **recalcitrant** about leaving the field after the coach removed him for a pinch hitter.*

- **malicious** (hateful, hostile): *In his next movie, John **Malkovich** plays a **malicious** character who holds up a bank and takes three hostages.*

- **filibuster** (long-winded oratory used to delay action): *Nobody can get a word in edgewise when Regis **Philbin** launches into a **filibuster** on a topic unrelated to the show to avoid having to do the weather report.*

- **vagabond** (nomad, wanderer): *James **Bond** portrays a vagabond traveling around the world to solve espionage schemes in the "shaken, not stirred" 007 series.*

- **billingsgate** (loud, foul insults): *The managing editor told the reporter, "You better hold your tongue and not hurl **billingsgate** at **Bill Gates** during your upcoming interview, just because you are having problems with your Microsoft software."*

- **catharsis** (gushing purification, cleansing): *Every morning at 10:00, I watch **Kathie Lee** undergo a catharsis—sometimes with tears, sometimes with tantrums.*

- **brandish** (make a threatening gesture): *I cringe when I watch Marlon **Brando brandish**ing a gun and wildly threatening the guards in* Apocalypse Now.

Psst! Is It "Lie" or "Lay"?

There are plenty of words in English that people regularly confuse. Some of them can be easily unraveled with a little practice. Here are twelve terms people frequently misuse. Commit these pairs to memory.

- **accept / except:** *Accept* means "to receive." *Except,* usually a preposition, signals "exclusion from a group or a unit," as in the sentence "I like foods *except* those seasoned with cumin." Consider, for instance, the statement *"The Attleboro Country Club will <u>accept</u> all new candidates <u>except</u> Sharon."*

- **affect / effect:** *Affect* is always a verb, one that means "change or influence." While *effect* can also be a verb meaning "produce, bring about, or make," it is most often a noun, meaning "the result or consequence." *High food prices affect the poor disproportionately in America, producing the worst effect on elderly people with fixed incomes.*

- **anecdote / antidote:** An *anecdote* is "a brief or amusing story," and an *antidote* is "a cure." *Sometimes the antidote for a dull party is, in fact, a humorous anecdote from someone like Great-Aunt Marge, the former Wild West rodeo bull-rider.*

- **could care less / couldn't care less:** Which is correct? When your neighbor tells you he just won $6 million in the lottery, you could wave him off and say, "*Oh, I couldn't care less*," meaning "It's absolutely impossible for me to care less than I do." "*I could care less*" is incorrect.

- **criterion / criteria:** The difference here lies between singular and plural. One requirement is a *criterion,* as in "*The criterion for membership is a check for $50.*" Two or more such requirements are *criteria,* as in "*All the criteria for membership can be found in the Bullmoose Bulletin.*"

- **imply / infer:** This is a difficult one. *Imply* means "suggest or hint," as in "*Do you wish to imply by making that face that my beef stew is bad?*" *Infer* suggests "a conclusion reached through reason and evidence," as in "*Let me infer from your ashen face and flop sweat that you don't like my beef stew.*"

- **its / it's:** Despite the strange and tortured things being done with apostrophes these days, this pair is still distinguishable. *It's* is the contraction for "it is." *Its* refers to "ownership." Consider, for example, "*It's clear that the cat lost its collar in the bushes.*"

- **lie / lay:** Remember *lie* means "recline" and *lay* means "put down." *You've been working hard. So for a moment, lie on the couch and lay your book on the floor. In the meantime, your cat will lie on your stomach or perhaps lay on your chest a special gift.*

- **phenomenon / phenomena:** Singular and plural again (oh, those Greeks). *John Travolta is a Hollywood phenomenon* (remember the movie?). *But hundreds of alleged sightings of alien aircraft around Roswell, New Mexico, add up to UFO phenomena.*

- **principle / principal:** Which one is your pal? Yes, it's the *principal*. A *principal* is either "the leader of a school" or the adjective meaning "the most important one." A *principle* is "a basic truth, law." *The principal member of the flute section has a cold and can't play the Beethoven piece tonight. The best principle for everyone is to tell the truth.*

- **regardless / irregardless:** Simple. There is no such word as *irregardless, regardless* of the number of people who insist on using the longer term.

- **sight / site:** A Web *site* is "a location," as is a construction *site*. But *sight* means "vision," as in the words *insight, oversight,* and *outtasight*.

- **unique / most unique:** *Unique* means "one of a kind." The term *most unique* doesn't compute because one-of-a-kinds (like Little Richard) can't be compared. Practice the correct term in statements like *"My boss's management style of compassionate tyranny is unique."*

Practice Exercise: Play Them As They Lie

To practice some of these problematic word choices, fill in the blanks below, choosing the correct form for the sentence.

1. Before you _____ down for a nap, _____ your jacket across the back of the couch. (lie / lay)

2. The most interesting _____ at Sea World are the performing killer whales. (phenomenon / phenomena)

3. If you'll _____ my advice on the Johnson contract, I think you'll find the next round of negotiations easier for everyone _____ Johnson. (accept / except)

4. The newspapers seemed to _____ that the coach of the Jets was unhappy with the offensive line. (imply / infer)

5. _____ of the cold weather, my daughter wants to go swimming at the YMCA this afternoon. (Regardless / Irregardless)

6. For certain, the best _____ to winter depression is lots of sunshine. Call the travel agency. (antidote / anecdote)

7. My only _____ for this position is a good work ethic. (criterion / criteria)

8. Frankly, my dear, I _____ if you want to see *Gone With the Wind* tonight. (could care less / couldn't care less)

9. The _____ aspect of life inside the Arctic Circle is the intensity of the aurora borealis light shows. (unique / most unique)

10. The best _____ for raising children is to maintain a sense of humor. (principal / principle)

ANSWERS: 1. lie, lay, 2. phenomena, 3. accept, except, 4. imply, 5. Regardless, 6. antidote, 7. criterion, 8. couldn't care less, 9. unique, 10. principle

It's Greek (and Latin) to Me

More than 80 percent of English words come from other languages, primarily Latin and Greek. In the course of borrowing and adapting from the ancient languages, English authors and speakers used some expressions again and again, creating long lists of related English words. For example, the Latin *anima* ("soul/spirit") gives us words like *animate*, *animism*, and *equanimity*. The Greek *anti-* (against) contributes *antiseptic*, *antagonist*, *antipathy*, and *antiperspirant*. A practiced word sleuth can use Greek and Latin clues to help unlock the meaning of difficult English words.

Look for examples from Greek and Latin in words you encounter on a daily basis. You'll find them in newspapers, on street signs, in work manuals. Wherever your eyes may wander, the linguistic *vestiges* (remains) of Athens and Rome are plentiful. Here are some Latin and Greek keys to help you expand your English vocabulary.

Word Building Blocks

Latin/ Greek	Meaning	Example
cent	one hundred	*centennial* (a hundred-year celebration)
chron	time	*chronometer* (exceptionally precise timepiece)
gen	to give birth	*generative* (capable of producing, originating)
gnos	knowledge	*prognosis* (forecast or prediction)
graph, gram	write	*epigram* (a written witticism, slogan, or joke)
gyn	woman	*gynecology* (the study of women)

Latin/ Greek	Meaning	Example (cont.)
homo	same	*homonyms* (different words with the same pronunciation)
logy	study of, science	*anthropology* (the study of humans)
loqu	speak	*eloquent* (possessed of articulate speech)
mal	bad	*malevolent* (hateful, hostile)
metr	measurement	*metrology* (a system of measurement)
omni	all	*omnivore* (someone who eats anything)
phon	sound	*cacophony* (loud clashing noise or noises)
poly	many	*polyglot* (someone who knows several languages)
pro	for, toward	*proponent* (one who is for a proposal or position)
psych	mind, soul, spirit	*psychotic* (mentally disturbed)
sequ	follow	*sequential* (following in order or time)
sub	under, below	*subliminal* (below the threshold of conscious perception)
super	above, beyond	*superlative* (above and beyond all others)
vert	turn	*vertigo* (dizziness, perhaps from turning)

Greek and Latin Roots for $500

Use your understanding of Greek and Latin roots to answer the following questions. Review the word building blocks above, then fill in each blank below with the word that seems appropriate.

a. intro<u>vert</u>

b. <u>cen</u>tenarian

c. meteoro<u>logy</u>

d. <u>psych</u>oanalysis

e. <u>sub</u>poena

f. ag<u>no</u>stic

g. dia<u>metric</u>al

h. <u>omni</u>potent

i. ana<u>chron</u>ism

j. <u>homo</u>phone

_____ 1. Something that is inappropriate for its era or unlikely for its <u>time</u>—like a World War I movie where computers are part of the scenery.

_____ 2. A word that <u>sounds</u> the <u>same</u> as another (for example, *bare* and *bear*) but has a different meaning.

_____ 3. A piece of paper that requires you to appear in court "<u>under</u> penalty of law."

_____ 4. Therapy and counseling for the <u>mind</u>, a treatment based on conscious and unconscious mental processes.

_____ 5. A skeptic, one who believes that certain <u>knowledge</u>, like religious belief, is unknowable.

_____ 6. The <u>study</u> of weather and weather patterns.

_____ 7. Someone who is shy and self-directed, someone who <u>turns</u> inside for entertainment and stimulation.

_____ 8. Two positions that, if <u>measured</u> against each other, are exact opposites.

_____ 9. A force that is <u>all</u>-powerful, such as a god or deity.

_____ 10. An increasing phenomenon in America, someone who is one <u>hundred</u> years old.

ANSWERS: 1. i, 2. j, 3. e, 4. d, 5. f, 6. c, 7. a, 8. g, 9. h, 10. b

Greek and Latin Roots for $1,000

Now let's look for some other English words that share the same ancient relatives as those above. Search the word building blocks for the following words. Then fill in each blank below with a word that seems to fit the clues.

a. <u>mal</u>adroit

b. <u>phon</u>ics

c. miso<u>gyn</u>ist

d. <u>poly</u>morphous

e. <u>graph</u>ology

f. <u>loqu</u>acious

g. <u>super</u>numerary

h. <u>pro</u>jectile

i. en<u>gen</u>der

j. ob<u>sequ</u>ious

1. A(n) _____ fellow has <u>bad</u> balance and poor small muscle control. In short, he's a klutz.

2. Hate speech tends to _____ racial ignorance and <u>gives birth</u> to other ills like racial prejudice and violence.

3. _____ is the educational method that teaches the relationship between spelling and <u>sound</u>.

4. Someone who is especially <u>talkative</u> is considered a(n) _____.

5. Someone who hates <u>women</u> is a _____.

6. The study of an individual's hand<u>writing</u> is called _____.

7. The movie extras <u>above</u> and <u>beyond</u> the number needed for the cast of *Ben-Hur* constituted a(n) _____ group that built sets for the movie.

8. In *The Hobbit*, Gollum is sometimes a(n) _____ fellow who <u>follows</u> Bilbo, but at other times he's a dangerous adversary.

9. Something that takes <u>many</u> forms, like Odo, the shapeshifting security officer on *Star Trek: Deep Space Nine*, is _____.

10. When little Alvin <u>throws</u> a baseball at the plate glass window next door, he is launching a(n) _____.

ANSWERS: 1. a, 2. i, 3. b, 4. f, 5. c, 6. e, 7. g, 8. j, 9. d, 10. h

Tip of the Day

One of the handiest little reference books in the world is a thesaurus. This popular book, a long-standing friend of writers and speakers, lists matches and near-matches for thousands of words. So if the words *sly moves* just aren't adequate to describe what your sneaky boss did to gain control of the company, a good thesaurus offers rich synonyms like *machination, artifice,* or *contrivance.* Here's another example. The student *feigned* a story to cover up not finishing his biology assignment. A thesaurus suggests alternatives such as *concoct,* or *fabricate.* There's most likely a thesaurus built into the word processing program on your home or work computer, and that's a helpful resource, too. But the pocket thesaurus— small enough to put in a purse or a jacket—is a useful companion for those long subway rides or short coffee breaks.

A word of caution: The thesaurus is a terrific tool. But, like so many indispensable tools, it can be overworked. Use appropriate restraint. Thumb through your thesaurus often. It is an invaluable resource—one you'll come to depend on. But don't use it to change *every* word in that memo, that letter, or that e-mail. Utilize your pocket resource to promote clarity, precision, and style. Those are the real goals of all conscientious writers and speakers.

In Day 2 you will discover, among other things, what your doctor is saying about your medical condition. What does it mean when your physician suggests *rhinoplasty* or *lipectomy*? Also you will look at words from Washington, those perplexing terms that politicians use when they don't want us to know what they're doing. Finally, you can look forward to learning ten ways to practice new vocabulary words.

Doctor, Do You Think He'll Be *Maladroit* Forever?

Learning New Words Every Day

This chapter illustrates several different strategies to add new words to your growing word database. By the end of the chapter, you will know the meaning of medical and political terms and ways to practice new vocabulary words. Remember, you need to say or write a new word several times to feel comfortable using it in verbal and written communication. Let's start by looking at Greek and Latin roots to lay the groundwork for learning medical terminology.

Key Terms to Enter Medical School— Where Does It Hurt?

When you visit your doctor, when you read about health issues, when you talk with Aunt Martha about her various operations, it's a real plus if you can use medical terms accurately. Whether you're trying to decipher the Explanation of Benefits form from your health care provider or HMO or leafing through the patient "literature" on a particular disease or condition in your doctor's waiting room, you will find that many of the words and terms used are based in Latin and Greek. Let's review some of the most important Latin and Greek roots that identify parts of the human body.

Word Building Blocks: Med School 101

Latin/ Greek	Meaning	Example
arthr(o)	joint	*arthritis* (inflammation of a joint)
cardi(o)	heart	*cardiac* (related to the heart)
carp(o)	wrist	*carpal tunnel syndrome* (wrist disorder)
cephal(o)	head	*encephalitis* (inflammation of the brain)
cyst(o)	bladder	*cystoscopy* (visual examination of the bladder)
cyt(o)	cell	*cytology* (study of cells)
dactyl(o)	finger or toe	*syndactylism* (fingers or toes joined together)
dermat(o)	skin	*dermatoconiosis* (irritation of the skin)
gastr(o)	stomach	*gastritis* (inflammation of the stomach)
hem(at)o	blood	*hemostasis* (blood not circulating)
hepat(o)	liver	*hepatic* (related to the liver)
hyster(o)	uterus	*hysterectomy* (removal of the uterus)
lip(o)	fat	*lipomyoma* (tumor containing fat tissue)
mast(o)	breast	*mastoplasty* (plastic surgery of the breast)
nephr(o)	kidney	*nephrology* (study of the kidneys)
oste(o)	bone	*osteopathology* (study of bone diseases)
phleb(o)	vein	*phlebotomy* (incision in the vein)
rhin(o)	nose	*rhinoplasty* (reconstructive surgery of the nose)

Pop Quiz: Where Does It Hurt?

Here are eight words. Your job is to figure out the meaning of each word using your word building blocks. Here's a hint for all you *nascent* (budding, new) medical students: *-itis* means "infection or inflammation of."

1. cephalitis
2. cystitis
3. phlebitis
4. nephritis
5. hepatitis
6. mastitis
7. rhinitis
8. dermatitis

Now that you have scanned the body parts (Med School 101), you're ready for Med School 201—terms for medical procedures or medical conditions. While the Greek and Latin roots determine which organ is under scrutiny, these suffixes help predict what medical treatment is involved.

Word Building Blocks: Med School 201

Suffixes	Meaning	Example
-algia	pain	*myalgia* (muscle pain)
-ectomy	removal, excision	*appendectomy* (removal of the appendix)
-emia	blood condition	*leukemia* (abundance of white cells in blood)
-itis	inflammation	*bursitis* (inflammation of the bursar sac)

Suffixes	Meaning	Example (cont.)
-metry	measuring	*cardiometry* (measuring heart function)
-oma	tumor	*melanoma* (malignant pigmented tumor)
-ortho	straighten	*orthodontia* (the straightening of teeth)
-osis	abnormal condition	*dermatosis* (disease of the skin)
-pathy	disease	*nephropathy* (kidney disease)
-plasty	plastic or surgical repair	*arthroplasty* (joint reconstruction)
-rrhexis	rupture	*angiorrhexis* (ruptured blood vessel)
-sclerosis	hardening of	*arteriosclerosis* (hardening of arteries)
-scopy	visual examination	*colonoscopy* (visual exam of the colon)
-spasm	twitching, contraction	*gastrospasm* (stomach contractions)
-statis	lack of movement	*metastasis* (condition beyond control)
-stomy	forming a new opening	*colostomy* (new opening in the colon)
-tomy	incision	*tracheotomy* (incision in the windpipe)

Pop Quiz: Do You Want an -Ectomy or a -Plasty?

Use your newly learned Latin and Greek building blocks to identify the nature of the medical procedure described below.

1. **Cytoscopy.** Should you prepare for an examination of your skin, cells, or wrist?

2. **Arthroplasty.** Are you destined to have space age metals in your teeth or your hips?

3. **Carpostatis.** Will you have trouble with your tennis game or your soccer skills?

4. **Cephalotomy.** Do you now have an extra hole in your heart, your breast, or your head?

5. **Nephroma.** Does this condition indicate a tumor on the bladder, kidney, or bone?

6. **Phlebectomy.** Have you lost a finger, a gland, or a vein?

7. **Arthralgia.** Should you rub Ben-Gay on your chest, your back, or your joints?

8. **Lipectomy.** After this operation, will you more likely be a size six or a size twelve?

ANSWERS: 1. cells, 2. hips, 3. tennis game, 4. head, 5. kidney, 6. vein, 7. joints, 8. size six

The Wordsmith: Context Clues

One of the wordsmith's favorite tools is the highlighter marker. It comes in handy while you're rumbling along in a commuter train, standing motionless in a glacierlike carpool lane, or waiting in a doctor's office. When things come to a standstill, pick a good magazine and mark the words you want to learn. Okay, so you're here at the clinic for a cholesterol count and your annual lecture on French fries. Reach over and grab a magazine to mark. *The Atlantic Monthly*? Good choice.

The Atlantic Monthly is published in Boston and retains a Boston flavor. The city's sixty-plus colleges and universities produce a highly educated populace. The *Atlantic* typically prints articles for a reader who lives in the Fenway, listens to the Three Tenors, reads novels like *Moby Dick,* vacations in Europe, and watches the Discovery channel. The magazine is truly wonderful, but even scanning the essay titles in the *Atlantic,* where words such as *devolution, trope,* and *nostrum* appear regularly, can require a thesaurus and an Advil.

An issue of the *Atlantic* featured "India's Grand Trunk Road" by Jeffrey Tayler, a travelogue description that begins at the Ganges River. Even if some of the words are obscure, Tayler's passage makes an impression, paints a picture. But you're also traveling on a word search today, one that requires your own brush strokes. So use that highlighter to mark the hard words—here's an example:

> *Across the emerald pool fell a shimmering image of lotus-shaped* cupolas *and copper*-gilt *walls.* Dhoti-*clad men lowered themselves on chains into the water to perform* ablutions; *women in* saris *murmured prayers in Punjabi. Such a domain of peace and piety—the Golden Temple, the* sanctum sanctorum *of Sikhism—had been impossible to imagine while navigating the* clamorous *lanes of Amritsar outside. The temple was orderly, efficient, with* gurus *on duty in shrines around its sides, and with Sikh bookstores and a museum of Sikh history at its entrance. Sikh guards, dressed in robes of* alabaster *white and turbans of royal blue, patrolled the chalk-soft marble walkways with spears, enforcing a discipline and* solemnity *foreign to places of worship elsewhere in India.*

You can see each new word is surrounded with context clues. For example, *dhoti* is followed by *-clad,* so you know it's an article of clothing. *Gurus* stand *in shrines,* implying a religious duty. *Alabaster* precedes *white,* denoting a quality of that color. So, there you have it: Sometimes the key to comprehending new words simply requires reading them in context. If you take note of a word like *alabaster* in a handful of different sentences, you can figure out its meaning and put the word to work. Let's see how well you do at unraveling context clues in the Ganges scene.

Words from *The Atlantic Monthly* for $500

Now it's your turn to see if you can find the meaning of the words below using the context clues from the reading passage.

1. ablution	a. cotton loincloth
2. alabaster	b. religious teacher
3. clamorous	c. cleansing
4. cupola	d. holiest temple
5. dhoti	e. noisy
6. gilt	f. smooth and white, perhaps translucent
7. guru	g. coated, often with precious metal
8. sanctum sanctorum	h. seriousness
9. sari	i. domelike structure
10. solemnity	j. long, draping outer garment for women

ANSWERS: 1. c, 2. f, 3. e, 4. i, 5. a, 6. g, 7. b, 8. d, 9. j, 10. h

Good work. Next to studying roots and suffixes, context clues are your most reliable way of understanding new words. Hanging on to this new knowledge is your next step. A helpful method is a *context card*. Before you leave the doctor's office, jot down on the back of your prescription paper the sentences with each of the words you want to save. (Of course, when you're reading something you can't actually highlight, like a library book, carry some 3x5 index cards with you and write down the word or words as you go.) When you get home, jot down the information from your scrap paper on a file card or type it into your computer, adding meanings and synonyms. You will need a dictionary.

Example: ablutions

- **Context:** "Dhoti-clad men lower themselves on chains into the water weekly to perform *ablutions*."
- **Meaning:** cleansing, often as a religious ritual, with water or liquids
- **Pronunciation:** (a-BLOO-shunz)
- **Synonyms:** washing, anointing, cleansing, purifying
- **Your own use in context:** "Jenny's ablutions create a traffic jam outside the bathroom door every morning."

"Take Two Aspirin and Call Me After Your Ablutions"

There's one final step: practice, practice, practice. As soon as possible and as often as possible, put your new words to use. That's the best way to stake out ownership. Well, how about writing a note to your doctor? For example:

Dear Dr. _____:

Recently, I visited your office for a checkup. I was struck by the solemnity of your advice. You are my health guru, and I appreciate your diagnosis. I will no longer make McDonald's my sanctum sanctorum. I must complain, however, about being stuck in the examination room for a half hour wearing only a robe that felt and looked like a dhoti. It was cold.

Sincerely,
Your Patient

Always go back and review your new words before sending the note. It's always a good idea to double-check until those new phrases become natural (you don't really have to send the note, of course—we're just practicing!).

Top Ten List: Great Strategies to Practice New Vocabulary Words

P.S. See if you can find some words you learned in Day 1.

1. **Send an e-mail.** Write somebody every day and use your new words. It's absolutely the easiest vocabulary practice available. Take advantage.

2. **Each day put self-adhesive notes with new words on things you encounter.** Carry a pad of those little note squares and use them to describe your world. When you find that psychedelic tie-dyed shirt in your closet, attach a Post-it that says "anachronism" (something out of its proper time in history). When the neighbors play country-western music at a zillion decibels, go to the mailbox and leave a note saying "cacophony."

3. **Start each morning with a different prefix as the daily theme.** If it's Tuesday, it must be *ob*-day. *Ob* is a Latin prefix meaning "toward," "to," "on," "over," and "against." In English, you also find the use of *ob* to capture the notion of "inversely," "reverse," or "against," as in *object* (I *object* to your adding so much salt in the stew). Then use as many appropriate words beginning with that prefix as possible before climbing into bed for the night. For example, *obdurate* (stubborn, immovable, pigheaded), *obfuscate* (confuse, befuddle, stupefy), *obligatory* (mandatory, necessary, required), *oblique* (evasive, devious, slanting at an angle), *obsequious* (submissive, flattering, unctuous),

obsolete (out-of-date, outmoded, old), *obtuse* (blunt, insensible, dull). Think, write, and speak them. Let's make Wednesday *ab*-day. *Ab* means "away from," as in *abatement. The accident created an <u>abatement</u> in our dinner plans, causing us to reschedule for another time.*

4. **Do you have a Scrabble set?** It's probably in the basement boxed up with Sorry! and Monopoly. Drag it out. Now put the game squares on your kitchen table or work desk—maybe even the coffee table. Every time you go by, arrange the squares to spell out new vocabulary words for the day. The action of spelling out the words should do good things for your memory and your word bank. Guaranteed.

5. **Make use of that blackboard, whiteboard, easel, or bulletin board at work.** Write or post your daily word list there. The simple act of declaring your interest in words helps you make a personal commitment to vocabulary growth. Besides, you might stir up some officewide interest in language: "Hey, Sally, what's this *concoction*? You must have spent hours mixing all the ingredients." Give it a try.

6. **Post your growing vocabulary list next to the phone.** When you make or receive a call, find a way to work one or two words into the conversation: "I'm sure your idea will be *lucrative*, Uncle Al, but my financial situation won't allow me to give you a loan." We all spend too much time on the phone. At least it can be beneficial to your word list.

7. **If you eat out frequently, it's a good opportunity to practice new words.** Admit to your dining companion that you *quail* at the prospect of eating at Mom's Diner. The next time you are at the coat check line, ask the attendant if that mink coat is real or *faux*.

8. **Write letters.** Find an excuse to write a letter, that ancient art of putting pen to paper. For example, today most of us grudgingly accept bad service and shoddy workmanship as part of living in the twenty-first century. It's time to rebel and speak out. You're *incensed* beyond expression and no longer willing to *capitulate* (you're mad as hell, and you're not going to take it anymore). Write a letter of complaint about the VCR that still won't track or the catalogue skirt that arrived with a tear in the seam. Use your *burgeoning* (growing or blossoming) vocabulary to get some action.

9. **Practice on your kids (or someone else's kids if you don't have any).** If they're teenagers, they already think you're from another planet, so a few puzzling phrases won't matter. Tell Evie to stop being so *recalcitrant* and just go clean her room. Tell little Sally Mae that her finger-painted "I love Mommy" card is the best *antidote* for a long and difficult day.

10. **Find friends who want to improve their vocabulary.** You can share new words every day. Maybe your friend is a co-worker, someone you phone a lot, or an e-mail pal. If so, you have unlimited opportunities to share the joy of discovering new words.

A Tour of Political Words

There is an entire lexicon of words that refer to politics, including the language of diplomacy, governance, and bureaucracy. Many of these words come from proper names, such as *czar,* a form of *Caesar.* Today a czar is an authority figure, as in the government's "drug *czar.*" Other Washington words come from Latin or Greek constructions (*covert, demagogue, xenophobia*—definitions follow shortly). Political terms often reach far beyond Capitol Hill to become metaphors for everyday life. For example, if you break up a battle between the Bickersons next door, you've reached a *détente* (peace) on Maple Avenue. If the IT (Information Technology) crowd at work is scheming for special privileges, the group is a *cabal.*

It's extremely useful to know the language of Washington. Current events keep you in touch with lawmakers and pending litigations, world events and trends, economic news and congressional policy. In Washington, the big players all use important key words.

Some words from Washington remind you to keep an eye on your elected officials. For example, a *boondoggle* is "work of little practical value," a term often applied to politically motivated projects. United States senators and representatives regularly embark on "fact-finding tours" at public expense, often to such political hot spots as Hawaii, Barbados, and Tuscany. These tours are known as *junkets.* Can you think of a mnemonic device to remember the meaning of *junket?* Some suspicious voters even believe that politicians enjoy a *sinecure,* "an office requiring little or no work." The word is easy to remember when divided into its Latin roots—*sine* and *cura,* meaning literally "without a care." For instance, some skeptical citizens have actually suggested that in America the office of vice president is a sinecure.

Key Terms from Washington:
A Pox on Jingoistic Demagogues

Here are some other political terms that regularly find their way onto the editorial and political pages of the newspaper.

They're words you will want to know and use. Read the sample sentences, then take the quiz that follows.

- **abdicate** (renounce the throne, an office, or a privilege): *In a famous moment of British history, King Edward VIII abdicated his throne to marry a divorced woman.*

- **barrister** (the British term for "lawyer," derived from the practice of standing before the "bar" in court): *When the trial began to look bad for his client, the barrister asked for a twenty-minute recess.*

- **caucus** (a closed meeting of political leaders to choose a candidate or platform): *In July, the Democratic caucus gathered to choose their candidate for the upcoming election.*

- **consensus** (a complete agreement, where everyone comes to a similar conclusion, usually at the same time): *Among the senators, there was consensus that national health care could be funded at the expense of the Social Security program.*

- **covert** (concealed, hidden, secret): *President Nixon's campaign of covert operations cost him the American presidency in the early 1970s.*

- **demagogue** (a popular orator who often uses social upheaval to advance politically): *The lobbyist for the tobacco industry acted as a demagogue inciting the crowd against tough new anti-smoking laws in California.*

- **dissident** (someone who disagrees with the prevailing opinion): *On the issue of gun control, those favoring disarmament of all Americans formed a dissident group, pitting members of the Republican party against one another.*

- **fascism** (a totalitarian and dictatorial rule): *European fascism was witnessed around the world when Hitler took absolute control of Germany.*

- **gerrymander** (draw voting boundaries for political advantage): The term *gerrymander* was coined in 1812 for Elbridge Gerry, governor of Massachusetts, whose state map featured a county border breakdown that looked to political cartoonist Thomas Nast like a salamander. Thus, the word *gerrymander* was born. *Governor Smith, a staunch Republican, gerrymandered the state's voting districts so that more GOP candidates would have the advantage on election day.*

- **hegemony** (leadership or dominance, usually unappreciated): *Richard Gere will tell you that China's hegemony over Tibet is unfair and tyrannical.*

- **plurality** (the number of votes separating winner and loser): *With the Reform party gaining strength in America, the plurality of votes in presidential elections is getting smaller and smaller.*

- **pundit** (a source of opinion, a critic, often political): *In Washington, the pundits who believe in campaign reform also believe that the Redskins will win the Super Bowl.*

- **quid pro quo** (fancy phrase meaning "this for that," "tit for tat"): During his term of office, President George Bush promised "No quid pro quo" and sent puzzled reporters all over America running for dictionaries. *The mediator suggested a quid pro quo arrangement with the two battling executives—a promise to clean up the toxic waste in exchange for the right to develop a contaminated one-thousand-acre parcel of land.*

- **Rubicon** (a point of no return): *Rubicon* also comes from Ancient Rome: When Caesar crossed the Rubicon River with his armies, he was committed to fight or perish. *In their decision to impeach the president, the Senate crossed a <u>Rubicon</u> with voters.*

- **schism** (a division into parties): *The <u>schism</u> between Reagan Republicans and liberal Republicans has widened in the past few years.*

- **solon** (a prestigious term for a political representative or legislator—and a reference to Solon, a wise and respected Athenian statesman): *In their final vote, the <u>solons</u> appropriated money for cancer research rather than for the B-2 bomber.*

- **xenophobia** (fear of foreigners): *A rising wave of <u>xenophobia</u> in the country encouraged Congress to adopt strong new immigration quotas.*

Pop Quiz: Terms from the Hill

Choose the answer that best defines each word below.

1. **demagogue**
   a. one who disagrees with the established opinion
   b. a representative of the people
   c. a popular speaker who can arouse a crowd

2. **barrister**
   a. a petty criminal
   b. a lawyer
   c. a member of the United States Congress

3. **consensus**
   a. feeblemindedness caused by old age
   b. agreement
   c. a population count that occurs every ten years in America

4. **abdicate**
   a. to speak in a loud and offensive tone
   b. to rule like a dictator
   c. to voluntarily give up an office or position

5. **dissident**
   a. one who disrespects others
   b. one who disagrees with others
   c. one who agrees with others

6. **covert**
   a. changeable
   b. concealed, hidden, secret
   c. not available

7. **fascism**
   a. totalitarian and dictatorial rule
   b. government by the people
   c. a government based on religious values

8. **solon**
   a. a senator
   b. a bureaucrat
   c. a high-flying official

9. **caucus**
   a. a dinner meeting on someone else's expense account
   b. a political meeting to choose a candidate or platform
   c. a division into parties

10. **schism**
    a. a division into parties
    b. a kind of bribery
    c. the exertion of unappreciated dominance

11. **pundit**
    a. a political commentator
    b. an outcast
    c. the kicker for a football team

12. **Rubicon**
    a. a point of no return
    b. the act of giving up an office voluntarily
    c. totalitarian rule

13. **plurality**
    a. the democratic process
    b. a political meeting
    c. the number of votes separating the winner and loser

14. **hegemony**
    a. a warning about political hot spots
    b. a voice of solemn authority
    c. exertion of leadership or dominance, usually unappreciated

15. **quid pro quo**
    a. "this for that"
    b. "Buyer beware"
    c. "What, me worry?"

16. **xenophobia**
    a. a fear of bad television shows
    b. fear of foreigners
    c. fear of politicians

17. **gerrymander**
    a. purposely misleading language
    b. to draw voting boundaries for political advantage
    c. to get out the vote on polling day

ANSWERS: 1. c, 2. b, 3. b, 4. c, 5. b, 6. b, 7. a, 8. a, 9. b, 10. a, 11. a, 12. a, 13. c, 14. c, 15. a, 16. b, 17. b

Brain Teaser

In his book *Word Play*, Maxwell Nurnberg recites a number of proverbs that he cleverly obscures as gobbledygook. Besides being fun, these twisted sayings offer a good chance to unsnarl the language and learn some new words. Let's try to translate a few from Nurnberg's extensive list. Example: Members of an avian species of identical plumage congregate. Answer: Birds of a feather flock together.

1. It is fruitless to attempt to indoctrinate a superannuated canine with innovative maneuvers.

2. Freedom from incrustations of grime is contiguous to rectitude.

3. Where there are visible vapors having their provenance in ignited carbonaceous materials, there is conflagration.

4. A revolving lithic conglomeration accumulates no congeries of a small, green bryophytic plant.

5. Missiles of ligneous or petrous consistency have the potential for fracturing my osseous structure, but appellations will eternally remain innocuous.

6. A plethora of individuals with expertise in culinary techniques vitiate the potable concoction produced by steeping certain comestibles.

Answers:

1. You can't teach an old dog new tricks.

2. Cleanliness is next to godliness.

3. Where there is smoke, there is fire.

4. A rolling stone gathers no moss.

5. Sticks and stones may break my bones, but words will never hurt me.

6. Too many cooks spoil the broth.

Now let's try reversing the process. Get out your thesaurus and translate the sayings below into obscure phrases. Then see if your family or friends can figure them out. Get extra credit for using some of your new words from these first two days or any new words you've recently mastered. I will get you started. For example, consider Alexander Pope's famous phrase "To err is human, to forgive, divine." With your thesaurus, you could change it to "Making fallacious decisions is typical of bipeds who use language, but offering general amnesty for offenses is the work of the Deity."

1. Spare the rod and spoil the child.

2. Brevity is the soul of wit.

3. A fool and his money are soon parted.

4. Beauty is only skin-deep.

5. The pen is mightier than the sword.

6. Let the punishment fit the crime.

Tip of the Day: A Potpourri of Word Play Web Sites

Don't be discouraged by the word *potpourri,* which once meant "rotten pot" in French and is reminiscent of Aunt Phyllis's Tuna Surprise casserole. Potpourri, of course, today suggests "a miscellaneous mixture," one that can be delightful, as in the fragrant potpourri you can buy in home furnishings stores. Such is the strange but wonderful Web site hosted by Judi Wolinsky called "Word Play: Sites That Feature Fun with Words." Log on to "Word Play" at www.wolinskyweb.com/word.htm for some playful approaches to word power.

Wolinsky's site stretches for many, many pages and provides listings for word nuts of all types. The collection includes some of these great destinations: "Amanda's Mnemonics Page," the "Anagram Hall of Fame," "Brit-Speak," "Burma Shave Signs," "Create Your Own Shakespearean Insults," "Country Western Song Generator," "Dillon's Online Vocabulary Tests," "Java Script Vocabulary Stretchers," "Investor Words," "Medspeak," "New Words in English," and "Words That Could Be Confusing/Embarrassing in the US and the UK." In "Word Morphs," you enter one word, and the host computer offers a list of new words differing by only one letter. In "Sounds of the World's Animals," you discover what French, Chinese, and Swedish cows say (it's not *moo*!). At the site called "Jennifer's Language Page," you learn how to say *hello* or *thank you* in Kurdish, Danish, or Portuguese (among others). If you are really interested in some weird word wackiness (or are a closet Trekkie), check out the Klingon Language Institute site, where Shakespeare and the Bible are translated into Worf's native tongue.

In the meantime, get ready for Day 3. I'll be offering you another pearl of wisdom from Mom, along with some nifty word lists that deal with people and personalities. Also included is a thought or two on how the newspaper can be a great resource for the enterprising wordsmith.

I Must Stop *Abnegating*

Practicing New Words Every Day

English is indeed a remarkable language, comprising close to a half million words, not including vast lists of technical and medical terms. Constantly you are washed by the seas of language, great waves of words that ebb and flow around you. On the average day, you encounter scores of new words, many of them useful and exciting. Don't ignore those new words: Embrace them, master them, use them! Every day the tide washes up a fresh new storm of words. The trick is to pay attention. Following are some special and helpful ways to open your eyes to new and wonderful words.

Good *Times:* Using the Newspaper As a Vocabulary Builder

> *"The* [New York] Times. *Our national treasure. Our Marilyn. Our Elvis. In other words: What We Have. People who complain murderously about the* Times *ought to be shot."*
>
> —George W. S. Trow

Apparently some people feel strongly about their daily newspapers. In an article in *The New Yorker*, essayist George W. S. Trow says that he grew up in New York in the 1930s surrounded by the city's many daily papers, including the *Sun*, the *Herald Tribune*, the *Daily News*, the *World-Telegram*, the *Journal-American*, and the *Mirror*. Each had its own distinctive audience. "I was told," says Trow, "that not to read the [*New York*] *Times* was to condemn oneself to second-class citizenship."

Even though most of these New York–based publications are now defunct, the *New York Times* endures, having established itself over the last century as arguably the most prominent newspaper in the world. For people like Trow, it remains a symbol of success, achievement, and status. Why?

Well, for starters, the *Times* offers a rich vocabulary. If you are serious about a more powerful vocabulary, reading a good newspaper like the *Times* is extremely helpful. Not only are the stories and columns informative and engaging, but the language is challenging.

So there you have it. Newspaper is destiny. You are what you read. In a real sense, that is a valid statement. Yes, there are other terrific newspapers, ones that can also augment and enrich your word bank. Buy those papers and read them! But since the *Times* finds its way to most American cities and, in fact, to cities around the world by bus, train, plane, and ox-cart, you can read it wherever you live. I appreciate its availability. You don't even have to subscribe to the *Times;* you can go online and read excerpts from the paper, or you can go to your local library.

Starting today, let's concentrate on ways to turn your morning coffee ritual into a daily vocabulary exercise. What do you like? Sports? The stock market? Fashion? Travel? It's all in the *Times*—and more. Turn to your favorite section and get started. Here are some reading hints.

Accent the Best New Words

In your kitchen nook, favorite coffee shop, or while riding public transportation, use your highlighter to mark up the *Times*. Look for interesting new words to highlight and practice. They're everywhere.

1. Today the young tennis stars Venus and Serena Williams travel "with their *ubiquitous* laptops." **Meaning:** The machines are ever present.

2. Americans' current interest in travel to exotic places like Transylvania seems "a unique *phenomenon*" to travel agents. **Meaning:** An unusual occurrence.

3. A Nobel Prize winner displays "a *capacious* brow" on his frowning face. **Meaning:** It's big.

4. An annual fee of $1,000 buys "a certain *cachet*" for American Express Centurion Card holders. **Meaning:** They have a high-priced seal of approval.

5. A new and unexpected trend in America is "*abnegation*, the practice of self-denial." **Meaning:** Some people are rejecting material goods and their pleasures.

Look for Words Already on Your List

By now, you've assembled a healthy list of new words, not only from this book, but from your important new role as a word-gatherer. Don't be surprised to find words like *entrepreneur* or *xenophobia* in sections of the paper like Sports, Travel, and Money and Business. Whenever you encounter a newly mastered word, spend a moment studying its context. When you first find these words in other settings, you will get an even better sense of their usage. Comparing contexts is an excellent way to commit a new term to memory.

Set a Goal

How many words can you borrow from the *New York Times* today? Aim for a daily goal of three or four. Remember, three new additions to your lexicon a day equals 1,095 words a year. That's impressive. Keep a notebook of your findings and practice them in verbal and written communications. Put all three into one big whopping sentence and try it on the waitress: "The *ubiquitous* fat-free latte may be an American *phenomenon*, but I think it's a *colossal* mistake." Copy your new words onto index cards (remember these from Day 2) or tear out the highlighted words and stuff them into your wallet. But don't leave that bistro without making a conscious effort to reach your word-gathering goal. You can do it!

The Top Ten Key Words from Greek Roots

In 1925, E. Y. Lindsay identified the most frequent Greek and Latin building blocks for English words. Below is a list of the Greek roots that contribute the most to our present-day vocabulary. With this basic list, you can decipher the meanings of hundreds and hundreds of useful English words. Consult the Greek models and use your word knowledge to complete the sentences that follow.

Word Building Blocks

Greek Roots	Meaning	Examples
anthrop	human or male	*anthropoid, philanthropic*
auto	self	*autocrat, autonomy*
bio	life	*biotic, symbiosis*
graph	write	*bibliography*

hetero	different	*heterogeneous*
homo	same	*homonym, homogeneous*
log	word, science, study of	*etymology, eulogy*
phil	love, friendship	*Anglophile, philander*
soph	wise	*sophisticated, sophist*
tele	far, distant	*telepathy, telekinetic*

Now, test your newly learned Greek roots to complete the following sentences (hint: some roots are used more than once in this exercise).

1. Transmitting thought waves across <u>distance</u> is called _____pathy.

2. A(n) _____oid creature is <u>human</u>like in build and movement.

3. A(n) _____isticated woman is worldly-<u>wise</u>, refined, and knowledgeable.

4. A(n) _____nym is a word that sounds and is spelled the <u>same</u> as another.

5. Before burial, a commemorative speech full of good <u>words</u> about the deceased is called a eu_____y.

6. Something composed of <u>different</u>, unlike elements or parts is _____geneous.

7. When you analyze Greek <u>words</u> that serve as English roots, prefixes, and suffixes, you are studying etymo-_____y.

8. _____geneous groups, which are composed of people with the <u>same</u> background, usually reach consensus more rapidly than heterogenous ones.

9. A man who <u>loves</u> many women without serious intention is a _____anderer.

10. A(n) _____crat rules or dominates without help and consults only him or her<u>self</u>.

11. Giving away money for the good of <u>humanity</u> is an act of phil_____ic generosity.

12. Giving a country or colony <u>self</u>-ruling power is called _____nomy.

13. _____omoric behavior is immature, not <u>wise</u>.

14. An Anglo_____ <u>loves</u> England and its cultural heritage.

15. When something is <u>alive</u>, like the layer of dirt in your teenager's closet, it is most probably _____tic.

16. A catalogue or list of <u>written</u> works at the end of a book is called a biblio_____y.

17. A person who can move objects <u>far</u> away or close up with his mind is _____ kinetic.

18. Any kind of relationship that is mutually beneficial for each of two <u>living</u> creatures is sym_____tic.

ANSWERS: 1. tele, 2. anthrop, 3. soph, 4. homo, 5. log, 6. hetero, 7. log, 8. Homo, 9. phil, 10. auto, 11. anthrop, 12. auto, 13. Soph, 14. phile, 15. bio, 16. graph, 17. tele, 18. bio

Key Terms: Minding Your ABC's at Cocktail Parties

So you're going to a cocktail party? A birthday bash? A summer solstice soiree? It sounds like fun. But it's also an opportunity to practice your growing word list. Here are some terms specially selected for debuting at a party. I think you'll find them fun and useful. Photocopy this list and stick it into your suit jacket pocket or handbag. Your first task of course is to have a good time and enjoy yourself. Second, use as many of these terms as possible. Speak well and with confidence. There's a term here for every letter of the alphabet. Good luck, you *terpsichorean* fool, you dancing machine. While you're scanning the list, *nota bene* (Latin for "note well") the number of borrowed and adapted French terms (more on French words in Day 7).

- **ambience:** atmosphere, decor, impression
- **banal:** trite, boring
- **coiffure:** a hairdo, usually a woman's
- **décolletage:** cleavage, but formally attired cleavage
- **ennui:** boredom
- **femme fatale:** a dangerous, alluring woman
- **gauche:** lacking social grace, awkward, "left-handed"
- **hors d'oeuvres:** appetizers
- **insouciance:** the ultimate calm, cool attitude
- **jovial:** happy, joyous, blithe
- **kitsch:** art or literature of dubious value
- **liaison:** a clandestine meeting (clandestine means secret)
- **malfeasance:** a crime, impropriety, or offense
- **n'est-ce pas:** a fancy tag line meaning "Isn't that so?" or "Don't you agree?"
- **oenophile:** a wine lover
- **panache:** style, class, distinctive manner
- **quixotic:** odd, eccentric, unusual, romantic in an impractical way, derived from the famous work *Don Quixote* by Miguel de Cervantes
- **renaissance:** a rebirth, a renewal
- **savoir faire:** social tact, refinement, grace, elegance

- **terpsichorean:** characteristic of dancing
- **urbane:** suave, polished, courteous
- **vapid:** uncool, unpolished, dull, tasteless
- **whimsical:** playful, fanciful, capricious
- **x-dividend:** a stock market symbol indicating an interest dividend (you'll see how this fits later)
- **yin and yang:** opposing life force principles—one positive, one negative
- **zest:** cheerful good humor, enthusiasm, relish

Following are sentences that use these words in context.

A is for ambience. Parties don't have atmosphere; they have *ambience.* At a noteworthy gathering, the marbled floors and distinguished oak wall paneling, the endless tables of delicacies, and the handsome well-dressed couples all contributed to a festive *ambience.*

B is for banal. Any cocktail party conversation involving pets, the weather, or recent surgical procedures will ultimately turn out to be *banal.* See how others react to the statement, "We can't decide whether to winter in Maui or the Côte d'Azur."

C is for coiffure. Try shocking your conversation partner by commenting that Lynda's *coiffure* reminds you of Marge Simpson's beehive hairdo.

D is for décolletage. As she entered from the balcony, you probably marveled at Marlene's designer gown, her ample *décolletage* decorated with a single *alabaster* (from Day 2) rose.

E is for ennui. "When Harvey turns on the sports channel," said Alicia with boredom, "I am filled with *ennui*. All I see is pucks, balls, clubs, sweat socks, and beer commercials. It's enough to put me to sleep."

F is for femme fatale. Everyone loves to talk about movies at parties. You might observe that Michelle Pfeiffer was a *femme fatale* when she portrayed Catwoman in *Batman Returns*.

G is for gauche. It is *gauche* to eat with your fingers and not use a napkin at a five-star restaurant.

H is for hors d'oeuvres. At a stylish affair, the *hors d'oeuvres* might include pepper-baked Brie, crab puffs, or even caviar. Lucky you—if this were at a Super Bowl party, you'd get Chee-tos and bean dip.

I is for insouciance. A studied lack of concern is the trademark of actors like Sam Shepard, Frank Sinatra, and Lauren Bacall. The dark, mysterious woman in the corner is practicing *insouciance*. Do not disturb.

J is for jovial. The word *jovial* is great for describing friends and acquaintances at parties because it suggests good humor, charm, likability, and acceptance. Your lively host, your delightful companions, even the uplifting atmosphere can be *jovial*.

K is for kitsch. If you like tasteless art, you'll love the *kitsch* exhibit at the Far West Popular Culture Conference. They're displaying prints like *Dogs Playing Poker* and *Velvet Elvis*.

L is for liaison. One of America's favorite movies about European manners is *Dangerous Liaisons*, starring Glenn Close and John Malkovich. It's an alluring tale of deceit and secret meetings that dramatically and poignantly define the term *liaison*.

M is for malfeasance. At a party, some people like to talk about the sins, crimes, and corruptions of others.

Remember, the official party word for crimes and misdemeanors is *malfeasance*, as in "John's *malfeasance* over the coffee kitty is now being referred to as Caffeinegate."

N is for n'est-ce pas. Saying this instead of "don't you agree" is so much more fun. Try this line at the Super Bowl party: "The Chee-tos seem especially fresh and crispy tonight, *n'est-ce pas?*"

O is for oenophile. As you ask for a glass of fine Fetzer Merlot instead of a beer, turn to your companion and explain, "I'm especially fond of good wines. I guess you could say I'm an *oenophile.*"

P is for panache. Gerry's parties are always done with such *panache*. Every guest receives a glass of champagne when arriving.

Q is for quixotic. Odd, whimsical (see below), or impractically romantic behavior is *quixotic* (remember Don Quixote tilting at windmills), as when Woody Allen takes his clarinet into New York City jazz clubs and sits down to play.

R is for renaissance. The *renaissance* of downtown Pittsburgh is a success story that involves urban planners, local special events, and community input. At the next party you attend, mention a part of your own city that has undergone a reawakening, a *renaissance.*

S is for savoir faire. Offering your dessert fork to an elderly woman who has dropped hers is an act of *savoir faire*. So is leaving the last *hors d'oeuvre* for another or picking up the check without a moment's hesitation. But the ultimate act of *savoir faire* involves slipping into the kitchen to help clean up after the fun.

T is for terpsichorean. Admittedly, *terpsichorean* is a word that's over the top, but let's try to work it in. When the music starts, you might have a chance to mention that you have almost no *terpsichorean* skills, but you'd be willing to dance anyway. The word often suggests a humorous style of taking to the dance floor.

U is for urbane. Many celebrities are described as *urbane* when they arrive at parties dressed in designer attire or take the time to sign autographs for fans.

V is for vapid. Spot the unsuave, unpolished, discourteous people at your party. Those who do or say things that are dull or tasteless may be called *vapid*— not to their faces, of course. That would indicate a lack of *savoir faire*.

W is for whimsical. A good party deserves a little whimsy. A lighthearted act of playful good humor is undoubtedly *whimsical*. For example, add a note of whimsy by bringing your yellow sticky notes (see Day 2) and labeling the scene. How about planting *kitsch* on the paint-by-number portrait or *femme fatale* on a sleeping Fluffy the Cat?

X is for x-dividend. Admit it. You thought I was going to suggest *xanthate* (a salt of a xanthic acid) or *xiphoid* (shaped like a sword). Nope. This one is useful. The word is *x-dividend*, the stock market symbol that says your little company, Terpsichorean Entertainment, Inc., which recently went public, is making a dividend payment. Yes, a cocktail party is an appropriate time to talk Wall Street and investments.

Y is for yin/yang. In Chinese philosophy, *yin* and *yang* are contradictory forces that interact to create order, balance, and meaning—as well as to determine fate.

Yin is dark, feminine, and negative. *Yang* is bright, masculine, and positive. Everything in life contains both *yin* and *yang,* the positive and negative forces that create Tao, the way of enlightenment.

Z is for zest. The word *zest* is doubly valuable at a cocktail party. It describes the hearty good fun and charming conversation (and the curly sliver of lemon peel in your cocktail). Doris spoke with *zest* about the band at her daughter's wedding reception.

Lessons from Mom: If You Can't Say Something Nice, Don't Say Anything at All

Mom, bless her heart, didn't like bad words. And when I got old enough to say my first really naughty one, she made it a memorable experience. Mom washed out my mouth with soap—not just any soap, but a particularly nasty-tasting one called Boraxo. It came in bar form, too, but Mom's instrument of torture was Boraxo soap flakes. They lathered up in no time.

After that, I carefully considered what I said, particularly about other people. Mom believed in the axiom, "If you can't say something nice, don't say anything at all." So, I learned to couch my criticisms in insults that sounded like compliments. I discovered that, with an appropriately articulate insult, I could express a full range of emotions, from mild displeasure to downright disdain—and nobody knew what I was really saying. It felt good.

That memory, however, doesn't mean I keep my mouth shut. In fact, I promptly speak my mind when a malcontent driver cuts me off on the expressway. But I always try to use words that Mom would approve, or at least ones that sound good while inflicting serious psychological damage.

So here goes. These are words to remember just in case you get stuck in traffic. And don't feel you have to wait until rush hour to practice. Surely there are some irritating people on the job, in the bank, at the mall, or in your face.

- **Censorious.** This word describes people who are "critical, complaining fault finders." When I was *censorious* of others, like my little cousin Susie, who never did anything right, Mom used to say, "Have you looked in the mirror lately?" Mom had a million zingers like this.

- **Doyenne.** This one is actually quite respectful, but there's a hidden insult here if you want it. A *doyenne* is the "eldest member of a group of women."

- **Jejune.** Here's another word that sounds like a compliment. Don't be deceived. *Jejune* means "dull, boring, and childish." The tattooed and body-pierced exhibitionists on music videos give new meaning to the word *jejune*.

- **Lugubrious.** This word means a "mournful or gloomy outlook (especially when exaggerated)." Team members had *lugubrious* expressions on their faces when they were told they didn't make the playoffs in the state championship hockey tournament.

- **Mercurial.** Describes someone whose attitudes or emotions "change quickly, suggesting a flighty, unreliable nature." John is so *mercurial,* he's constantly changing his mind about finding a new job.

- **Poltroon.** "A weakling, a coward." A favorite Renaissance insult was the epithet "poltroon." Brian acted like a *poltroon* when he wouldn't stand up for himself against the school bully.

- **Sanctimonious.** "A holier-than-thou attitude." The word *sanctuary* shares the first five letters with *sanctimonious,* offering you a mnemonic aid in remembering this useful word. Televangelists, especially when they are cataloguing other people's sins, tend to be *sanctimonious.*

- **Soporific.** Something that makes you sleepy is *soporific,* as in "Hey, Ned, thanks for that presentation on glue gun safety. It was really *soporific*!"

- **Sycophant.** Someone who "engages in endless flattery." The drudge who follows the boss and nods approval of every utterance is a *sycophant.* When the new hire told the boss that he'd work late "just because the office feels like my home away from home," everyone knew that George had replaced Betty Jane as the company *sycophant.*

- **Unctuous.** Means "oily." *Unctuous* people are smooth (in an unattractive way), smug, and insinuating. Sally described Linda's personality as *unctuous* after she managed to get World Series tickets from her boss.

- **Vainglorious.** The adjective *vainglorious,* which sounds regal and complimentary to someone whose word bank isn't up to snuff, means just the opposite—"self-absorbed, not treating others with respect." Mom would never let me call anyone "conceited" or "pompous," but *vainglorious* means the same thing. That self-important person who is always too busy to accept your calls or return your e-mail is probably *vainglorious.*

Brain Teaser

So far, we've learned several Latin and Greek roots. Here's a quiz to help you review those building blocks and add some new words at the same time. Study the following two lists of Latin and Greek roots below and then fill in the blanks with roots that are appropriate to the English word's meaning.

Latin and Greek Roots for $500

1. anthrop	8. gnos
2. anti	9. graph/gram
3. auto	10. gyn
4. bio	11. hetero
5. cent	12. homo
6. chron	13. log
7. gen	14. logy

Latin and Greek Roots for $1,000

1. loq	8. pro
2. mal	9. psych
3. meter	10. seq
4. omni	11. soph
5. phil	12. sub
6. phon	13. super
7. poly	14. tele

1. _____*scient,* a word meaning "all-seeing, all knowing."

2. *Philo*_____*ist,* one who loves words and studies them.

3. *Syn*_____*ize* means to set all clocks to the same time.

4. _____*ologist,* a scientist who studies human beings.

5. *Pro*_____*ticate,* a word meaning "to <u>know</u> before the fact, to predict."

6. *Dialecto*_____, the <u>study</u> of differing languages and dialects.

7. *Holo*_____, a three-dimensional image or likeness <u>written</u> on film by laser.

8. _____*technical,* a trade school having <u>many</u> courses in technology.

9. *Eu*_____*ious,* having a good <u>sound</u>, like wind chimes.

10. _____*motion,* a <u>self</u>-moving mechanical figure like a robot.

11. *Andro*_____*ous,* having male and <u>female</u> characteristics at once.

12. _____*logue,* the beginning speech or text that comes <u>before</u> the main part.

13. _____*communication,* the act of communicating over <u>distances</u>.

14. Like Dr. Sigmund Freud, a scientist of the <u>mind</u>— better known as a _____*otherapist.*

15. *Anti*_____*tics,* drugs that kill bacteria in <u>living</u> things.

ANSWERS: 1. Omniscient, 2. philologist, 3. synchronize,
4. Anthropologist, 5. prognosticate, 6. dialectology,
7. hologram, 8. Polytechnical, 9. euphonious,
10. Automaton, 11. androgynous, 12. Prologue,
13. Telecommunication, 14. psychotherapist, 15. antibiotics

Pop Quiz: "We Have Nothing to Fear but *Phobophobia* Itself"

Everyone is afraid of something. What's your specialty? Here's a long list of fears (*phobias*) that trouble people. When your co-workers show a squeamishness about insects (*ento-mophobia*) or animals (*zoophobia*), you'll be able to use just the right word to identify their anxiety. When your husband or wife starts complaining about turning permanently gray, you can say "Oh, honey, you've got *geraphobia*" (fear of old age).

Sometimes the technical term can salvage an embarrassing moment or avoid a tedious argument. For example, instead of explaining to the instructor of your night class, "The dog ate my homework," you might simply say, "I suffered a bout of *logophobia* (fear of study)."

Fear	*Meaning*
ailurophobia	fear of cats
arachnophobia	fear of spiders
gamophobia	fear of marriage
graphophobia	fear of writing
gymnophobia	fear of nakedness
gynephobia	fear of women
heliophobia	fear of sunlight
hippophobia	fear of horses
hydrophobia	fear of water
iatrophobia	fear of doctors
lalophobia	fear of speech
nyctophobia	fear of darkness
ochlophobia	fear of crowds
ophidioiphobia	fear of snakes
pantophobia	fear of everything
pedophobia	fear of children
peniophobia	fear of poverty
phasmophobia	fear of ghosts
pyrophobia	fear of fire
synophobia	fear of togetherness
thanatophobia	fear of death

Fear	*Meaning*
tomophobia	fear of surgery
triskaidekaphobia	fear of the number 13
zoophobia	fear of animals

Quizophobia!

It's time to practice the word building blocks from Days 1, 2, and 3 by trying your hand at these fictional phobias—some agonizingly real, others less likely to be found in medical books.

1. **Anthrophobia**   fear of _____
2. **Chronophobia**   fear of _____
3. **Gnosiophobia**   fear of _____
4. **Hemophobia**   fear of _____
5. **Herpetophobia**   fear of _____
6. **Lipophobia**   fear of _____
7. **Logophobia**   fear of _____
8. **Philophobia**   fear of _____
9. **Rhinophobia**   fear of _____
10. **Musophobia**   fear of _____

ANSWERS: 1. people, 2. time, 3. knowledge, 4. blood, 5. reptiles, 6. fat, 7. words or speech, 8. love, 9. noses, 10. mice

Tip of the Day: Minimizing the *Ubiquitous*

With the possible exception of the word *thing,* the most overworked word in the language is probably *get.* Usually the word is a lazy alternative to a clearer, more precise word or expression. Here are some sample sentences where the word *get* clearly needs some help.

- Please *get* a frozen pizza at the Shop-n-Go.
- Please *purchase* a frozen pizza at the Shop-n-Go.

- We wanted to *get* the house for less than $700 a month.
- We wanted to *rent* the house for less than $700 a month.
- Sally *gets* tired easily.
- Sally *tires* easily.
- Millburn *gets* no interest from his loan to cousin Barry.
- Millburn *earns* no interest on his loan to cousin Barry.

Make a note to notice how often *get* pops up in conversations—and especially monitor the times you use *get* in your own speech. Sometimes this overused word is the best choice ("I can't *get* home until noon"), but in most instances, *get* sounds weak, general, and inexpressive. Try to live without it. And if you're successful, start working on *thing* as well!

In Day 4, you'll look at famous names and the ten most frequent Latin roots. You'll also spend time looking at word pairs that people commonly confuse. I'll see you then.

Day 4

Why Is My Pet So *Petulant*?

Using New Words

In Day 3, you looked at the ten most productive Greek roots and how they contribute to English word formation. Now it is time to return to the Romans. Here is E. Y. Lindsay's list of the ten most frequently occurring Latin roots and some derivative English words. With this list, you can expand your knowledge of English considerably.

Top Ten Latin Roots

Review the list below and commit the roots and their meanings to memory. You will need them for a later exercise.

Latin Roots	Meaning	Example
cap	take, hold	*captivate* (attract, hold, enchant, lure)
cip	take, hold	*precipitate* (hasten, expedite, bring on)
cept	take, hold	*perception* (knowing, understanding)

Latin Roots	*Meaning*	*Example (cont.)*
fac	make, do	*facile* (done with ease)
fic	make, do	*efficacy* (efficiency, competence, success)
fect	make, do	*defect* (abandon, forsake, withdraw)
fer	bear, carry	*vociferous* (loud, insistent, distracting, "a voice that carries")
fin	end, limit	*infinite* (without end, limitless)
mit	send, throw	*emit* (send out, discharge, pour forth)
miss	send, throw	*emissary* (a messenger, a delegate, one sent to negotiate)
mise	send, throw	*surmise* (infer, throw out a guess)
reg	arrange, straighten	*regimen* (diet, health plan, arrangement)
rect	arrange, straighten	*rectify* (straighten out, correct, remedy)
ress	arrange, straighten	*redress* (adjustment, compensation, "straightening things out")
sta	stand	*stalwart* (standing firm and resolute, stout)
stat	stand	*statuesque* (graceful, regal, standing tall)
sist	stand	*desist* (stop, yield, relinquish, quit, stand down)
spe	look, see	*specious* (misleading, deceptive, incorrect)
spect	look, see	*prospective* (approaching, anticipated)
spic	look, see	*perspicacious* (observant, shrewd, clever, insightful)
ten	hold	*tenacious* (clinging, unyielding, steadfast)
tent	hold	*detention* (hindrance, delay, holding back)
tin	hold	*retinue* (group, band, accompanying troupe)

Latin Roots	*Meaning*	*Example (cont.)*
tain	hold	*retainer* (prepayment, held for later use)
vid	see	*provident* (cautious, prudent, seen as thrifty)
vis	see	*vis-à-vis* (face-to-face, in direct comparison)

Latin Roots for $500

For each of the sentences below, fill in the Latin root that successfully completes the word and fits the contextual meaning. Your clue is the underlined word. Note that some of the underlined words reflect two Latin roots (for example, "hold" could refer to *cap* or *ten*).

1. Someone who <u>stands</u> upright, with an elegant figure, a regal appearance, and a noble bearing may be called _____uesque.

2. A re_____ue is a group, a throng, or a crowd that <u>holds</u> the space around a leader, like a king's loyal advisers.

3. To <u>look</u> with a shrewd, careful eye and <u>see</u> everything clearly is to be per_____acious.

4. When you compare two professionals _____à_____, like watching Andrea Bocelli and Luciano Pavarotti sing the same aria, you can <u>see</u> similarities and differences in style.

5. Ralph Nader, who <u>holds</u> popular opinions on ecology and industry, is a _____acious fighter for environmental causes.

6. At the teachers' meeting, the principal asked all the teachers to _____ify an error in the daily bulletin, one

that they needed to <u>straighten</u> out before the students arrived for classes the next morning.

7. John's voci_____ous outbursts about the new wage scale contracts <u>carried</u> from one end of the union hall to the other.

8. A _____ile argument is one that a speaker can <u>make</u> without much effort. It's easy and comes naturally to the speaker.

9. Shelly Mae was able to _____tivate the crowd and <u>hold</u> their attention completely with her lyrical rendition of "Flow Gently, Sweet Avon."

10. When you <u>arrange</u> your food lists to include healthy fruits and vegetables, you are engaging in a _____-imen that will make you feel better and achieve optimum health.

11. Completing work on time and without wasted effort is the hallmark of great ef_____acy—what successful people <u>do</u> in this company!

12. In our world, people seem to think there is an in_____ite supply of clean water, a <u>limit</u>less fountain without beginning or <u>end</u>, but they are sadly mistaken.

ANSWERS: 1. sta**tu**esque, 2. re**tin**ue, 3. per**spic**acious, 4. **vis-à-vis,** 5. te**nac**ious, 6. **rect**ify, 7. vo**cif**erous, 8. **fac**ile, 9. **cap**tivate, 10. **reg**imen, 11. ef**fic**acy, 12. in**fin**ite

Latin Roots for $1,000

Let's challenge your knowledge of Latin roots with the sentences below. Complete as in the exercise above.

1. Someone who <u>stands</u> firm in his defense of human rights is described as _____lwart.

2. In order to obtain a lawyer's services—to <u>hold</u> a position on the attorney's docket of cases—you may need to pay the attorney a cash re_____er.

3. For the Japanese-Americans who suffered through the internment camps in World War II, the government's attempt to red_____ the situation through an <u>arrangement</u> of a $20,000 payment is a classic case of "too little, too late."

4. New cars <u>send</u> far fewer pollutants into the air these days, probably because the Environmental Protection Agency demands that vehicles e_____ a minimum amount of noxious gases.

5. No longer is it necessary for Russian athletes to formally de_____ from their homeland in order to <u>make</u> a new life in the free world.

6. In the twentieth century, painters like Salvador Dali and Pablo Picasso were able to <u>hold</u> their subjects under a different light, to see the world with their own unique per_____ion.

7. Wait! Stop! De_____! <u>Stand</u> away from the last piece of chocolate cake! It's part of my new diet regimen.

8. A(n) _____ious argument is one that anyone can <u>see</u> is misleading and foolish.

9. The president decided to <u>send</u> his e_____ary to meet with other delegates to discuss cultural affairs.

10. Pro_____ive employers will want to <u>look</u> through your résumé, especially searching for experience in their field.

11. Anatole took a pro_____ent view of life, <u>seeing</u> the many opportunities to save money on simple necessities like toothpaste.

12. Becky couldn't help but to sur_____ that the main character in the mystery novel survived the car explosion after she <u>guessed</u> that he switched identities with his brother.

ANSWERS: 1. stalwart, 2. retainer, 3. redress, 4. emit, 5. defect, 6. perception, 7. Desist, 8. specious, 9. emissary, 10. prospective, 11. provident, 12. surmise.

Key Terms: Famous Names

One of the most common terms in English is *guy.* But few people know that the broad circulation of this word comes from an important event in English history, one involving the unfortunate *Guy* Fawkes. In 1605, Fawkes and other members of a *cabal* were arrested while trying to blow up the Houses of Parliament, leading to a Protestant celebration known as Guy Fawkes Day—and finally to the popularization of the term "a regular *guy*" in both England and America. A great number of common terms like *guy* come from people's names. Below are some useful words that trace their origins back to famous people from history, mythology, and literature. Knowing the story behind each word helps you remember the meaning.

- **bowdlerize** (remove completely any questionable passages): Bowdlerizing is the prudish weeding out of any mildly objectionable passage from a book, letter, or document. In the nineteenth century, Thomas Bowdler spent his time and efforts editing Shakespeare's plays, removing all the puns and sexual references. *Before the PTA meeting, the principal <u>bowdlerized</u> any reference to school violence in the year-end school report.*

- **boycott** (a protest involving inaction): In 1880, an Irish land agent named Captain Charles Cunningham Boycott raised rents. In protest, the tenants organized a rally, so that no one in town would sell or provide the captain food or services. *Orchestrated by César Chávez, the famous American grape boycott in the 1960s resulted in millions of pounds of grapes rotting on the vines in California.*

- **chauvinistic** (fanatically loyal): Nicolas Chauvin was wounded seventeen times in the Napoleonic wars, but his injuries only reinforced his patriotism. Thereafter, he began praising Napoleon in such exaggerated detail and style that people began to laugh. Later, two French playwrights used the soldier's name in parodies, playing on the foolish way that Chauvin had fawned over the Little General. Chauvinism is a foolish—often outrageous or exaggerated—devotion to a cause. *Tom's chauvinistic devotion to the Flat Earth Society made him look foolish in the eyes of his colleagues.*

- **galvanize** (motivate into immediate action): In the eighteenth century scientist Luigi Galvani performed experiments with electricity and frogs, producing and studying the twitching reactions. Today, the term means "produce a quick result." *Carmen's flyer galvanized the neighbors on her block to complain about the plan for installing high-tension power lines.*

- **gargantuan** (enormous, gigantic): In 1532, French author Rabelais published his wild and sometimes frightening legends about a giant named Gargantua. From that point, anything huge or imposing has been called *gargantuan. Melvin's gargantuan appetite for pizza meant that everyone else could count on getting only one piece.*

- **maverick** (a nonconformist, a rebel): When every other rancher in frontier Texas was branding his cattle, Samuel A. Maverick obstinately refused. *The young independent candidate was considered a political <u>maverick</u> because he was fighting against the increase in school taxes.*

- **procrustean** (demanding conformity through arbitrary methods): The Greek highwayman Procrustes tortured his victims by tying them to a bed. If their feet were too long, he lopped them off. If too short, he stretched them out. *The country club had <u>procrustean</u> standards for each new member.*

- **puckish** (devilish, impish, playful): Puck is the troublemaking sprite in Shakespeare's *A Midsummer Night's Dream.* A puckish attitude is naughty and mischievous. *Jonathan had a <u>puckish</u> grin on his face when his mother discovered her burnt bathroom rug.*

- **sadistic** (cruel, perverse): During the French Revolution, the Marquis de Sade was a degenerate who used torture on those he loved. Sadism involves taking joy from inflicting pain. *Arnold played a <u>sadistic</u> joke on James by telling his friend that the Boston Red Sox had just signed Ken Griffey, Jr., to a long-term contract.*

- **vandalize** (destroy property, create a nuisance): The Vandals were a savage Germanic tribe that harried Europe and attacked Rome in the fifth century. *After three unsuccessful attempts to <u>vandalize</u> the school by destroying the science lab, the gang decided to target a nearby park.*

Quiz: Famous Names

It's time to practice new terms derived from proper names. Correctly match the vocabulary word with its definition. Remember, if the definition doesn't seem to fit your word choice exactly, don't try to make it work. That's a *procrustean* attempt!

1.	to startle into immediate action	a.	vandalize
2.	enjoying something sad, sick, perverse, or cruel	b.	gargantuan
3.	enormous, gigantic	c.	maverick
4.	to destroy property	d.	sadistic
5.	a protest, like refusing to buy food at the school lunchroom	e.	puckish
6.	playful, devilish	f.	procrustean
7.	to edit out questionable parts	g.	chauvinistic
8.	unreasonably and foolishly loyal	h.	galvanize
9.	willing to force conformity	i.	bowdlerize
10.	a rebel, a nonconformist	j.	boycott

ANSWERS: 1. h, 2. d, 3. b, 4. a, 5. j, 6. e, 7. i, 8. g, 9. f, 10. c

The Wordsmith: Rhyming and Similar-Letter Definitions

In Day 1, you worked with mnemonic devices, ideas, and strategies that help you remember words and definitions. Sound associations or spelling cues can also serve as mnemonic devices. They can be powerful tools for language building. Consider the following examples.

- **aborigine** (original inhabitant): *Their cultural origins suggest that the people called Australian aborigines were the earliest settlers of the land.*

- **bucolic** (relating to quaint rural life or quiet countryside): *The crickets and owls combined in a bucolic nocturne that made the residents of the little hamlet happy.*

- **condole** (join in mourning, express sympathy): *When both Bob and Elizabeth Dole failed to become president in separate campaigns, their friends wished to condole both husband and wife.*

- **dearth** (lack of, scarceness): *A dearth of food and water can readily and quickly cause death.* Note the similarity in spellings.

- **imbroglio** (a rumble, a fight): *Some comments about Paddy's Irish brogue started the wild imbroglio among two groups at an Irish pub.*

- **lecherous** (lewd, sexually charged): *"Yes, we're teenagers in love, but that's no reason to lecture us about sex!"*

- **peccadillo** (minor offense, slight fault, like using the wrong fork): Driving through the great Southwest? Those slow-moving animals you see are armadillos. Is there a word association clue here? Yes. *It's a peccadillo to bring your armadillo to a dinner party, without an invitation.*

- **petulant** (irritable, whining, annoying attitude): *My pet Plato is petulant about his new dog food and has been whining in the corner all afternoon.*

- **purloin** (steal): Sound association can help you to remember *purloin,* another word for the infamous "five-fingered discount." *Imagine Fagin, a well-known thief, at the local market, where he is stuffing a huge steak into a backpack. That's right, he's there to <u>purloin</u> a sir<u>loin</u>.*

- **rectitude** (honesty or conduct led by moral principles): Note the *-tude* in *rectitude,* a reminder of a moral person's honest atti<u>tude</u>. *The newspaper article described Liz's actions as recti<u>tude</u> after she followed her heart and adopted six homeless puppies that were about to be put to sleep.*

- <u>vac</u>**uous** (empty, unintelligent, unaware): *A <u>vac</u>uous person is empty-headed, almost as though the sense has been <u>vac</u>ummed from his or her brain.*

Pop Quiz: Rhyming and Similar Letters

Let's see how your word association skills are developing. Recall the sound or spelling cues above to help you identify the meaning of each word.

1. **peccadillo**
   a. Italian dry salami
   b. minor offense, slight fault
   c. irritable, whining, annoying attitude

2. **purloin**
   a. steal
   b. barbecue
   c. shop for bargains

3. **condole**
   a. to cut short
   b. vain and gorgeous male
   c. to join in mourning, express sympathy

4. **dearth**
   a. lack of, scarceness
   b. a rumble, a fight
   c. evil warrior prince

5. **vacuous**
   a. capable of easy cleaning
   b. empty, unintelligent, unaware
   c. honesty or conduct led by moral principles

6. **lecherous**
   a. covered with leeches
   b. lewd, sexually charged
   c. prone to giving advice

7. **imbroglio**
   a. an art form
   b. fumigation
   c. a rumble, a fight

8. **aborigine**
   a. an original inhabitant
   b. a minor offense
   c. the last item in a series

9. **bucolic**
   a. related to quaint rural life or quiet countryside
   b. easy and happy
   c. feverish and congested

10. **petulant**
    a. unpredictable attitudes
    b. pessimism
    c. irritable, whining attitude

11. **rectitude**
    a. being unaware
    b. honesty or conduct led by moral principles
    c. right-handedness

ANSWERS: 1. b, 2. a, 3. c, 4. a, 5. b. 6. b, 7. c, 8. a, 9. a, 10. c, 11. b

Five Ways to Build Your New Vocabulary on E-mail

Here are five ways you can increase your word bank in e-mails to your friends, family, and co-workers. Be on the lookout for vocabulary words from this section and earlier chapters.

1. **Write thank-you notes.** What did you get for your birthday from Uncle Bob and cousin Sal? A Popeil Pocket Fisherman? Terrific. Have you written your thank-you notes? I didn't think so. Here's a chance to use e-mail to *redress* that oversight and practice your word bank as well. "Dear Uncle Bob, although I have been remiss in thanking you for the Pocket Fisherman, I am truly thrilled. I can't wait for the *prospective* report on the upcoming fishing season!"

2. **Create reunions.** Old friends and schoolmates have a way of showing up on e-mail after long periods of silence, probably because your name gets out there on the Net in scores of ways that are hard to imagine. When that annoying Billy Bob from the Class of '83 drops you a "Hi there!" don't just press the delete button. Send off a newsy blurb with enough lies, exaggerations, and *specious* tales to make him wish he had not put gum in your ponytail in the sixth grade. "Well, Billy Bob, my diet and exercise *regimen* has me in good shape for the Olympic trials. I only hope that the demands of my Fortune 500 company will not force me to *defect* from the big meets this summer."

3. **Clean out your e-mailbox.** Use some big words to remove yourself from junk e-mail lists, the messages that create an *infinite* supply of unreadable and

unwanted e-clutter in your e-mailbox. "Dear Insurance Company of Peoria: Despite your persistence, I don't want to consider your whole life plan *vis-à-vis* my current policy. Please stop the e-mails. Quit! Cease! *Desist!* I have a lawyer on *retainer.*"

4. **Got kids?** Few of us have the time for all those school programs, teacher-parent conferences, and PTA meetings, even though we know we should be there. Well, e-mail was invented to *rectify* such problems—to keep you in contact with Maybelle's teacher or Janelle's principal. Almost every teacher in America has an e-mail address. Ask for a progress report. Look into your daughter's homework schedule. Find out if she's been a cooperative student. "Do you think that my daughter's *vociferous* behavior in the classroom has contributed to the *demise* of her scholarship?"

5. **Use e-mail at work.** You should have scores of chances every day to use your word bank online. For example, send e-mail suggestions to your boss and co-workers using new words. Outline the *efficacy* of the current budget plan. Offer your *perception* that the company Web site needs some bells and whistles if it is to *captivate* browsers: "If we remain *perspicacious* during the new year, we will see some golden opportunities to expand our e-commerce sales in the overseas markets."

Was Marilyn *Ravenous* or *Ravishing* at the Party?

In English there are scores of word pairs that people commonly confuse. For instance, if Marilyn is extremely hungry, she is *ravenous*. If she is enchanting and beautiful, she is *rav-*

ishing. If you want to compliment Marilyn's appearance and style, choose wisely. Here are some other word pairs that you should commit to memory.

- **alumnus / alumna / alumni:** If you earn your diploma from East Orange School for Girls, are you an *alumnus,* an *alumna,* or an *alumni*? Congratulations, young woman. You are an *alumna*. Confused? Blame those Romans (again). Pay attention. An *alumnus* is "a male graduate"; an *alumna* is "a female graduate"; *alumni* are "graduates (plural) of either gender."

- **between / among:** It's the Christmas season, and your present is a big box of dark chocolates. If you choose to share that box of candy with your uncles, aunts, and cousins, are you distributing the goodies *between* relatives or *among* relatives? You're spreading the candy *among* the relatives. The preposition *between* implies "the number two." *Among* is reserved for "three or more." Therefore, if you give candy only to Uncle Sal and Aunt Marie, you've divided the goodies *between* relatives. If you offer some to Aunt Jill as well, you've shared the candy *among* relatives.

- **censure / censor:** If you want to remove objectionable scenes from a movie, do you want to *censure* or *censor* the film? You want to *censor* it. *Censure* means "an expression of blame or disapproval." *Censor* is a "person authorized to examine literature, plays, or other material and who may remove or suppress what he or she considers morally or otherwise objectionable." The Church Lady wants to *censor* all the violent scenes from Oscar-winner *American Beauty,* but Al, the local movie critic, merely wants to *censure* the film, letting his fans know he thinks it's overrated.

- **compliment / complement:** Does a fine Cabernet
  Sauvignon *complement* a prime rib entrée or does the
  wine *compliment* the main course? The wine
  complements a good meal. Wine, candles, dessert—
  things that *complement* a meal—make it complete. A
  compliment is "praise or commendation." Give the chef
  of a superb meal a *compliment.*

- **dessert / desert:** Sahara, Gobi, Mohave. Where are
  you? Are you traveling through a *dessert* or a *desert*?
  Take extra water. You're traveling in a *desert,* "an arid,
  sandy region." If you're traveling in a *dessert,* take extra
  whipped cream. You'll need it for the berry pie, hot
  fudge sundaes, and tapioca pudding.

- **disinterested / uninterested:** The local police have
  arrested you for disturbing the peace. Do you want a
  judge in the courtroom who is *disinterested* or
  uninterested? Clearly you want a judge who is
  disinterested. An *uninterested* party is "detached,
  uninvolved, possibly bored." A *disinterested* group is
  "unbiased, detached, and fair"—a jury.

- **emigrant / immigrant:** In the movie *Born in East L.A.,*
  Cheech Marin is being illegally deported from Los
  Angeles in a citizenship snafu. Does this eviction from
  the United States make Cheech an *emigrant* or an
  immigrant? Cheech is an *emigrant.* "One who enters a
  new country" is an *immigrant,* while "one who departs
  for a new country" is an *emigrant.*

- **fewer / less:** To lose weight in this drive-through era,
  you must increase your activity level and decrease your
  calorie totals. If you reduce your food intake by 20
  percent each day, are you consuming *less* calories or
  fewer calories? On your new diet, you are consuming
  fewer calories. Anything you "can count" is described

by the adjective *fewer*, while "uncountable objects" are described by the word *less*. For instance, your gorgeous new body will be *less* bulky, and your face will have *fewer* chins.

- **grisly / grizzly**: Is the scene of an eight-car pileup on the freeway likely to be a *grisly* or a *grizzly* scene? This car crash scene is *grisly*, meaning "bloody, disgusting, and shocking." A *grizzly* scene would feature "large, ill-tempered bears."

- **hippie / hippy**: Before Susan began her diet, was she described by friends as *hippie* or *hippy*? Susan was *hippy* before her diet program. *Hippy* refers to "big hips." The word *hippie*, however, refers to "the psychedelic, tie-died, Grateful Dead devotees of the 1960s."

- **illusion / allusion**: Do Las Vegas magicians Siegfried and Roy create a world of *illusion* or a world of *allusion* with their smoke, mirrors, and disappearing Bengal tigers? Siegfried and Roy are masters of *illusion*. An *illusion* is "a deception, a mirage, a fantasy." An *allusion*, however, is "a casual reference, one that calls to mind the original event." In a media interview, Siegfried and Roy *alluded* to the fact that they consider their tigers and cubs to be their children.

- **ingenious / ingenuous**: Your sister bought an expensive outfit, and she asks your opinion. If, instead of evading the issue, you tell the truth, saying it's "out-of-date and frumpy," are you being *ingenious* or *ingenuous*? Shame on you. You're being *ingenuous* with your sister, who wants a compliment, not the truth. *Ingenuous* means "naive, candid, sincere," while *ingenious* means "brilliant, imaginative, skillful." Your sister was looking for an ingenious comment, not an ingenuous one.

- **loose / lose:** You convinced all your relatives to eat those Christmas goodies, and your pants are starting to look saggy. Good for you. Did you *lose* weight or *loose* weight? You were able to *lose* weight. *Loose* is an adjective meaning "not fastened or restrained," and *lose* is a verb meaning "rid oneself." When you *lose* weight, your clothes will become *loose*.

- **me / myself:** Which is correct? (a) "For myself, the anchovy-onion pizza is too spicy." (b) "For me, the anchovy-onion pizza is too spicy." The answer is *b*. *Myself* is appropriate in reflexive sentences like "I *myself* do not like anchovies" or "When I'm by *myself,* I usually order pepperoni." In these utterances, there's already a reference to the speaker ("I"). If there's no such added reference, *me* is appropriate. "To *me,* fishy pizza seems inedible."

- **passed / past:** Was the controversial Senate bill on gun control *passed* by voice vote or *past* by voice vote? The bill was *passed*. The word *past* is an adjective referring to "a bygone time, *past* events, *past* holidays, *past* circumstances." *Passed,* of course, is a verb. "The committee *passed* its budget."

- **pray / prey:** Does the hunter consider the white-tailed deer the *pray* or the *prey*? Bambi is the *prey*. Wise deer hunters *pray* for good weather and for the sobriety of their hunting friends who stalk their *prey* in the same dark woods.

- **prostate / prostrate:** If you find yourself face-down in the mud after a disagreement with a woman with quick reflexes, are you lying *prostate* or *prostrate* in the goo? You are lying *prostrate* in the mud. *Prostrate* means "lying prone or stretched out." A *prostate* is "a gland in males composed of muscular and glandular tissue that surrounds the urethra at the bladder."

- **try and / try to:** Is it better to say that everyone should *try to* improve their vocabulary skills or *try and* improve vocabulary skills? Everyone should *try to* improve those skills. The phrase *try and* is not grammatically correct, yet its widespread use is mind-boggling. Always *try to* use the correct form.

Tip of the Day

Grandma had a wonderful house. In spring and summer, it was full of flowers, and the rest of the year she scattered bags of *potpourri,* a dried mixture of sweet-smelling herbs. But the best part was the big coffee table in the front room. Only one object sat on the table: the dictionary.

The dictionary had a wealth of pictures and drawings, a book that challenged the mind and delighted the senses.

I still remember fondly the hours spent looking through the dictionary. It was too big for me to lift. I simply sat on the overstuffed couch. At the end of my visit, I walked away with a head full of new discoveries like *absinthe,* "a perennial aromatic European herb"; *grog,* "an alcoholic liquor"; *parsimonious,* "excessively sparing or frugal"; and *tumescent,* "becoming swollen, swelling."

There's something magical about a house where words take center stage. Over the years I saw friends, relatives, playmates—even Grandma's housekeeper—thumbing through the Big Book with looks of awe and reverence.

For those who want to know more about words, I recommend Grandma's choice. Buy a big, beautifully illustrated dictionary with heavy bold print and a rich leather cover.

Clear away everything else and let the book stand alone—opened to a favorite word—on the coffee table with plenty of good lamps nearby. Change the page frequently.

At this point in your ten-day course, you should begin to see some progress in your vocabulary skills and study methods. Remember, it takes three or four uses of a new word to give it a permanent place in your brain, so practice, practice, practice.

Tomorrow you'll encounter key terms from science, and the ten most difficult words to pronounce (and what they mean).

Day 5

How Do You Say *Gaucherie*?

Pronunciation and Other Word Strategies

As you conclude the first half of your vocabulary study, you should recognize some new and expedient ways to study. By now, I hope you're using the newspaper and other reading material to find new words, then practicing them in phone conversations and featuring them in e-mails. Also you should increasingly recognize the Latin and Greek components in English words, using these ancient word building blocks as keys to understanding. Finally, looking for mnemonic devices will help you remember what you've learned. Keep these hints in mind as you launch into Day 5.

Key Prefixes from Latin: *Ad-* to *Trans-*

Now that you have a firm grasp of key Latin and Greek roots, let's consider the top ten Latin prefixes, those helpful linguistic road signs that come at the beginning of English words. Here is a list of the most prominent Latin prefixes and some English derivations. As you read the sample words, notice how many others you could add from your own working vocabulary.

Prefix	Meaning	Examples
ad-	to, toward	*adieu* ("farewell," from the French for "to God")
		adduce (to bring forward, to the front, such as presenting evidence)
		addendum (something added to the original)
com-	together, with	*commingle* (mix together)
		complicity (a partnership, usually in crime)
		compress (press together)
contr-	against	*contralateral* (originating on an opposite side)
		controversy (a dispute between two sides holding opposing views)
		contravene (go against, oppose, resist)
de-	from, down	*depose* (remove from high office or position of authority)
		decant (pour from the bottle or container—wine, for example)
		deplete (decrease or exhaust the supply)
dis-	from, apart, away	*disembark* (land ashore, depart from a ship)
		disrepute (low regard, falling from favor)
		discordant (disagreeable, harsh, not pleasant to the ear)

Prefix	Meaning	Examples (cont.)
ex-	out, from, away, former	*expatriate* (someone banished, thrown out of the country)
		extinct (gone, died out)
		excise (remove, erase, amputate)
in-	not	*indolent* (not diligent, lazy, idle)
		inscrutable (not knowable, mysterious, secret)
		intemperate (not moderate, unreasonable, extreme)
in-	into	*indoctrination* (brainwashing, harsh instruction)
		incarcerate (imprison, confine, jail)
		infuse (introduce, ingrain, instill)
pre-	before	*predilection* (preference, a bias held before the final choice)
		preconceived (presupposed, assumed, prejudged)
		predisposed (prejudged, inclined to an opinion beforehand)
trans-	across	*transitory* (changeable, temporary, passing)
		transcend (exceed, leave behind, go beyond)
		transcribe (copy, rewrite, duplicate)

Exercise: Using Latin Prefixes

For each Latin prefix below, think of a word and sample sentence that captures the meaning of the prefix—perhaps several words. Note that a prefix may have more than one meaning. For instance, *defenestration* means exiting _from_ a window, while *deceleration* is the _opposite_ (negative) of *acceleration*. For best results, contribute a word for each meaning of the prefix. Have fun and be aware of how many words you already know for each Latin prefix. This exercise, done with some thought and effort, will help you unscramble words with similar Latin beginnings.

_____ 1. A word beginning with *ad*. Example: *advocate,* meaning "to give support <u>to</u> a goal or a position." *During the zoning board meeting, Sue said, "I <u>advocate</u> the removal of all hydroelectric dams on the Columbia River."*

_____ 2. A word beginning with *com*. Example: *comrade,* "one who goes <u>with</u> you on difficult or meaningful journeys." *The two <u>comrades</u> survived the Persian Gulf War.*

_____ 3. A word beginning with **contr**. Example: *contraband,* "material that is <u>against</u> the law to transport or <u>against</u> the rules to possess." *Before the Homecoming Game, the principal stood at the entrance gate and watched for <u>contraband</u> such as alcohol and firecrackers.*

_____ 4. A word beginning with **de**. Example: *depose,* "remove someone <u>from</u> office or <u>from</u> a position of authority." *The nobles <u>deposed</u> the king by stripping his power.*

_____ 5. A word beginning with **dis**. Example: *disparaging,* "<u>reduce</u> in esteem or rank." *Emily's <u>disparaging</u> remark had a negative affect on Kate's self-esteem when she told Kate she wasn't good enough to make the cheerleading team.*

_____ 6. A word beginning with **ex**. Example: *exfoliate,* "peel <u>away</u> the surface or top layers." *The cosmetologist prepared a dressing to <u>exfoliate</u> the rough skin from Christine's arms and shoulders.*

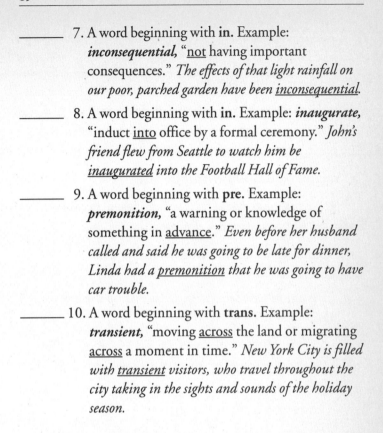

_____ 7. A word beginning with **in**. Example: *inconsequential,* "<u>not</u> having important consequences." *The effects of that light rainfall on our poor, parched garden have been <u>inconsequential</u>.*

_____ 8. A word beginning with **in**. Example: *inaugurate,* "induct <u>into</u> office by a formal ceremony." *John's friend flew from Seattle to watch him be <u>inaugurated</u> into the Football Hall of Fame.*

_____ 9. A word beginning with **pre**. Example: *premonition,* "a warning or knowledge of something in <u>advance</u>." *Even before her husband called and said he was going to be late for dinner, Linda had a <u>premonition</u> that he was going to have car trouble.*

_____ 10. A word beginning with **trans**. Example: *transient,* "moving <u>across</u> the land or migrating <u>across</u> a moment in time." *New York City is filled with <u>transient</u> visitors, who travel throughout the city taking in the sights and sounds of the holiday season.*

"Apostrophes Drive Me Crazy!"

Some of the smallest things in life can be the most annoying. Take apostrophes, for example, those funny little punctuation marks that show up in the strangest places when people think they're supposed to write proper English. Why do apostrophes puzzle so many people? Well, they are sometimes used to make plurals from letters, as in *P's* and *Q's*, or *ABC's*. But folks tend to generalize these rare instances, adding 's to plurals indiscriminately. At my local grocery store, I expect great buys on *potato's, avocado's,* and *peach's,* according to the erroneous hand-lettered signs. But I'd rather buy *potatoes, avocados,* and *peaches.*

Apostrophe use is a problem, I admit. But here's a good rule to follow: *If you don't know for sure whether to use an apostrophe, leave it out.* It's much better to delete the curious little digit than to use an apostrophe to form a plural incorrectly.

Practice Round: Apostrophe Use

Right or wrong? Make corrections when necessary, but leave the correct sentences as they stand.

1. Trembling with fear, I ate my cousin *Sylvia's* cheesecake.

2. Two union *member's* suggested a vote on the overtime issue.

3. When you find my purse, see if my *key's* are still inside.

4. *Bess's* mother wants me to leave a 20 percent tip for the service.

5. The *womens'* meeting ran late.

6. A *fishs'* mouth is usually soft and pliable.

7. Remember that your *dentist's* receptionist wants you to call.

8. The *dentists'* convention has been postponed until after Halloween.

9. I'm not sure that *papayas* color is a good sign.

10. The sale on *papayas* at Food For Less is really spectacular.

ANSWERS: 1. correct, 2. members (when in doubt, leave it out!), 3. keys, 4. correct, 5. women's (This is one of those plurals that doesn't end in *s.*), 6. fish's, 7. correct, 8. correct, 9. papaya's, 10. correct

"Did You Enjoy the Exhibits at the Art *Saloon*, Mrs. Malaprop?"

In the famous British comedy *The Rivals*, by Richard Brinsley Sheridan, Mrs. Malaprop is a character who habitually twists her words. Since 1775, such a linguistic *faux pas* has been called a *malapropism*. If your friend uses the word *saloon*, "a tavern," when she means *salon*, "a gallery or reception room," she is participating in this sometimes amusing confusion.

Below are some commonly confused word pairs, ones that might show up as malapropisms if you're not careful.

- **adverse / averse:** *Adverse* means "unfavorable" or "contrary." *Averse* means "reluctant" or "opposing." *An <u>adverse</u> condition, like a snowstorm, is contrary to safe driving and unfavorable for travelers. If you ask me to drive in a blizzard, I will admit that I am <u>averse</u> to the idea.*

- **avocation / vocation:** *Avocation* is "an activity added to one's regular work or profession." *Vocation* is "a regular occupation." *In his spare time Robbie took up sailing; his wife called it his <u>avocation</u>. After receiving a degree in finance, Judy knew her <u>vocation</u> would be investment banking.*

- **canvas / canvass:** *Canvas* is "cloth, fabric," the material of tents, sails, and tote bags. To *canvass* is to "solicit votes, lobby for candidates, or seek donations." *Troy bought a <u>canvas</u> on which to paint his masterpiece for the art show. The group in favor of Social Security reform <u>canvassed</u> the neighborhood, asking residents to support their cause.*

- **continuous / contiguous:** Events that are *continuous* are "ongoing" (like the arrival of junk mail). *Contiguous* things lie "in physical contact." *Marge could not abide the <u>continuous</u> laughter of the man sitting behind her in the movie. When geographers refer to the <u>contiguous</u> states, they mean ones that touch, sharing a common border, like North and South Dakota.*

- **covert / overt:** Total contradictions. *Covert* is "secret, obscured, and shadowy." *Overt* is "open, obvious, and uncensored." *Richard Nixon's <u>covert</u> operations team cost him the White House, even though he had previously gained great popularity with his <u>overt</u> political gestures toward China.*

- **credit / accredit:** As a verb, to *credit* means "trust" or "accept." To *accredit* is "certify." *Visa agreed to <u>credit</u> Barbara's account for an extra $50 after she proved that the pet-grooming charges were fraudulent. If you are taking classes, they are probably offered by an <u>accredited</u> institution, such as New York University.*

- **decisive / incisive:** Anything *decisive* is "conclusive, convincing, absolute." *Incisive* means "sharp, cutting, severe." *The West's struggle against communism produced a <u>decisive</u> political victory. Your sharpest teeth are the incisors, and your sharpest witticisms are <u>incisive</u>.*

- **deprecate / depreciate:** *Deprecation* is "belittling or insulting," as in *"Try not to <u>deprecate</u> my paint job unless you want a very colorful shirt." Depreciation* is "the devaluation" that typically occurs, for example, immediately after you drive that new Land Rover from the lot.

- **displace / misplace:** To *displace* something is to "move it." To *misplace* something is to "lose it, at least temporarily, or to put it in the wrong location." *If I pick up the red ceramic vase and move it from its normal spot on the shelf, I have displaced the vase. I can (and often do) misplace my checkbook.*

- **dissemble / disassemble:** *Dissemblers* are people who "confuse the issue, conceal the truth, or mislead those who listen." To *disassemble* something, like the vacuum cleaner, is to "take it apart." *The newspaper called the agency executives dissemblers for designing a new ad campaign that misleads clients about the risks. Joseph disassembled his Lego building and built a brand-new model.*

- **eminent / imminent:** *Eminent* is a synonym for "distinguished" or "noteworthy." *Imminent,* on the other hand, is an adjective meaning "coming soon" or "near at hand." *Stephen Hawking, author of* A Brief History of Time, *is an eminent scientist, a leader in his field. If you fail to pay your taxes, trouble with the IRS is imminent*.

- **final / finale:** Both of these terms refer to "the last event or decision." Observe the subtle differences. *Final* is an adjective; *finale* is a noun. The *finale* is "the final act, the conclusion, the denouement." *Nancy was nervous about being the final speaker because she knew it was her responsibility to end the conference on an upbeat note. The circus finale ended with the performers gathering in the center ring for applause.*

- **flout / flaunt:** *Flaunting* is a "showy display," as when the Tinseltown stars parade past the awestruck crowds on Oscar night. People in Hollywood often like to *flaunt* their good looks, fancy cars, and expensive clothes. On the other hand, *flouting* is a "mocking contempt," typical of drivers who openly disregard speed limits or handicapped parking signs. *Mildred decided to flaunt her new Mercedes, driving hell-bent down the carpool lane. In the process, she managed to flout the law against single-passenger travel during rush hour.*

- **incredible / incredulous:** *Incredible* means "unbelievable, outstanding, remarkable." *Incredulous* means "unbelieving, dubious, questioning." *The critics say Kevin Spacey is an incredible actor. If you can't believe he is both the hero and villain in the movie* The Usual Suspects, *you are incredulous.* While characters, objects, or events can be *incredible,* only people can be *incredulous: "I am incredulous that you would consider selling your incredible VW Bug for $1,200."*

- **motive / motif:** *Motive* is "a reason, a rationale, or an incentive." A *motif* is "a theme." *Police suspected Sharon's motive for robbing the bank stemmed from the fact that she had recently been fired from her job and couldn't pay her bills. In Shakespeare's plays, light and darkness are common motifs.*

- **negligent / negligible:** Everyone knows that *negligent* driving is "careless and thoughtless." *Negligible* is harder to remember. It means "insignificant, unimportant, or trivial." *Charlie's negligent attitude toward table manners cost him a chance for a second date with Phyllis. Before the new millennium, the Internet had a negligible effect on commerce in China.*

- **opaque / transparent:** Easily confused, *opaque* and *transparent* are nonetheless opposites. *Opaque* objects "don't let light through," but *transparent* ones "do let light through." *Because Joanna put the casserole in an opaque container, Patrick couldn't tell if it was tuna or chicken with rice. Kim used transparent paper to see the picture she wanted to trace for her art project.*

- **set / sit:** People *sit* down, but they *set* objects down. *Set* also describes the "act of placing anything in position," as in *"The pilot hesitated to <u>set</u> the manual on the control panel."* It's accurate to say that *"Kansas <u>sits</u> in the fast lane of Tornado Alley"* and that *"a big twister can <u>set</u> a tractor on a Wal-Mart rooftop."*

- **subsequently / consequently:** *Subsequently* simply means "later." *Consequently* means "as a result of." *When its football stars were arrested before the Big Game, Gator State University couldn't hold a meaningful practice. <u>Consequently</u>, they lost the big game with Southern Mississippi University. <u>Subsequently</u>, however, the players were released on bail.*

- **tortuous / torturous:** *Tortuous* means "twisting, winding, and full of turns." The word *torturous,* which looks similar to *tortuous,* means "painful." *At Big Sur, the Coast Highway snakes in a <u>tortuous</u> path along the rocky shores. Reverend Smiley's <u>torturous</u> sermon on the Good Samaritan was painfully long and rambling.*

Malaprop Quiz, Part I

To test your grasp of words from the Mrs. Malaprop section, fill in each blank with a word that suits the meaning and the context.

1. Before you decide to _____ your standing in the top five list of sales representatives, you'd better be sure you're not talking to someone who made the top four. (flout / flaunt)

2. To deflect blame from himself, Brendon began to _____, suggesting at the same time that Marge had stolen the Pop-Tarts. (dissemble / disassemble)

3. My agent's barblike attacks in the meeting were so
   _____ and severe that the executive types rewrote my
   book contract in ten minutes. (decisive / incisive)

4. Which of the following do you consider the most
   _____ and painful—an attack by fire ants or a night
   of karaoke at the club? (tortuous / torturous)

5. Yes, I spent my bus fare on a great big piece of red
   velvet cake at Angelo's House of Desserts. _____,
   I had to walk home in the rain. (Subsequently /
   Consequently)

6. The Healy family, who traveled from Europe for the
   wedding, were _____. They couldn't believe it when
   they heard the bride and groom were going to Asia for
   their honeymoon. (incredible / incredulous)

7. Since the artist drew all the cartoons for the book, the
   publisher gave _____ to the illustrator on the book's
   jacket cover. (credit / accredit)

8. Those inconsiderate people who use their cellular
   phones while driving on the expressway are _____ in
   their responsibilities to other drivers. (negligent /
   negligible)

9. Mary waited at the airport for the _____ arrival of her
   husband's plane, due in less than ten minutes. (eminent
   / imminent)

10. Please _____ your hat on the counter instead of
    throwing it onto the floor. (set / sit)

ANSWERS: 1. flaunt, 2. dissemble, 3. incisive, 4. torturous,
5. Consequently, 6. incredulous, 7. credit, 8. negligent,
9. imminent, 10. set

Malaprop Quiz, Part II

Okay, let's practice. Each sentence has at least one silly word. Find the mistakes and substitute appropriate terms from the Mrs. Malaprop section.

1. Regina decided to study welding and told her friend, "I hope to make ironwork my vacation."

2. When asked if she would consider chairing the executive committee, Colleen replied, "I am not reverse to the idea."

3. Standing at the service counter, Chuck asked, "Do you have a manual on how to dissemble a Jiffy Job vacuum cleaner?"

4. When Madeline, wearing only a nightgown, was stopped for speeding in a school zone, the officer said, "Sorry, lady, I've got to cite you for negligee driving."

5. The bank robber, wearing an outlandish pink outfit, confessed to the crime, saying, "My motif should be clear. I need a new wardrobe."

6. "I really hate to accredit Bill with having fixed the computer," said Larry. "In fact, I think that another crash is eminent."

7. Grabbing an obnoxious pink and green pullover sweater, Gary yelled to his wife, "Alice, you won't believe the incredulous bargains on this table!"

8. When the ballet reached the two-hour mark, Dudley, who'd been twisting in his chair the whole night, said, "This *Swan Lake* stuff is tortuous, Mabel."

9. When he finished rolling his best game of the year, Benny turned to the bowling team and said, "Hey, on the way home, let's stop for a beer at that new salon on Fifth Street."

10. "Collecting antiques is my new hobby," said Charlene. "I needed a new allocation because I was getting tired of working all the time."

> ANSWERS: 1. vocation (vacation), 2. averse (reverse), 3. disassemble (dissemble), 4. negligent (negligee), 5. motive (motif), 6. credit (accredit) + imminent (eminent), 7. incredible (incredulous), 8. torturous (tortuous), 9. saloon (salon), 10. avocation (allocation).

Top Ten List: The Most Difficult Words to Pronounce (And What They Mean)

If your basement holds a box full of *Hooked on Phonics* tapes, you probably believe that English spelling and pronunciation have something in common. You dreamer, you. Why is English spelling so divorced from pronunciation? Collisions with the Romans, the Vikings, the French-speaking Normans, and others helped to wrench English spelling from the systematic to the absurd. But the truth remains, whatever the causes, there are some odd combinations of letters out there, sometimes in words that you will find useful. Here's my top ten list.

1. **bourgeois** (boo ZHWA): Means "typical of middle-class values, perhaps boringly so." *After spending a month with her wealthy aunt, Lynn's bourgeois attitude became more sophisticated as she learned all the proper social graces.*

2. **connoisseur** (kon uh SOOR): Is an expert in the arts or in manners, one who appreciates fine taste and has the qualifications to make critical judgments. *Martha Stewart (to some, anyway) is a connoisseur of fine dining and decoration.*

3. **denouement** (da noo MAHN): Is the "end, the final act, the conclusion." *For the Bears, who lost eight games in a row, the final game against the Packers was simply the <u>denouement</u> to a long winter of discontent.*

4. **gaucherie** (GO shuh ree): Be careful. It's "social awkwardness," like putting your elbows on the table or sticking your napkin under your chin. *When Reynaud embarked on a series of bird calls during the intermission of* La Traviata, *his wife, who was embarrassed by his <u>gaucherie</u>, took a cab home.*

5. **heinous** (HEY nuss): Means "awful, terrible, horrifying." *The Holocaust in Nazi-occupied Europe represents for many the most <u>heinous</u> aspects of humanity.*

6. **inchoate** (in KO ate): Means "just begun" or "incomplete." *Something in its first stages is inchoate. Phil's understanding of physics is <u>inchoate</u>. He's just beginning to get the idea that light is both a particle and wave.*

7. **oblique** (o BLEEK): Means "slanting or indirect—not straightforward," perhaps even devious. *The salesman's <u>oblique</u>, evasive answer about the ingredients in Fashion Model Hand Cream, made Jennifer wary of the company's entire line of beauty products.*

8. **soupçon** (SOOP sahn): Means "a trace, a suspicion, a flavor." *Just a <u>soupçon</u> of garlic is the secret to Peggy's Perfect Chicken Wings.*

9. **usury** (YOO zhu ree): "An outrageous rate of interest" is usury. *Today many check-cashing shops charge 30 percent interest or more, a kind of <u>usury</u> that is sometimes called "predatory lending."*

10. **Weltanschauung** (VELT an show en): Refers to "a person's worldview." *The Weltanschauung for many rock stars is best described as "Show Me the Money!"*

Quiz: Fill in the Blanks

Now take your newly learned words and complete the sentences below.

1. After Edward wore his motorcycle jacket to the Junior Prom, an incredible act of social tactlessness, his _____ became legendary at Ridgemont High.

2. Instead of being direct and forthright, the candidate took an _____, standoffish position on physician-assisted suicide, saying he thought it was a matter for the courts to decide.

3. In Martha Grimes's *Rainbow's End,* Detective Inspector Jury has three murder cases to solve and only a(n) _____ of evidence—an almost infinitesimal amount.

4. Sometimes _____ middle-class activities like barbecues and Bingo games are just the right antidote for the dull midsummer's evening.

5. The most _____ crime of the 1990s was probably the horrifying wave of genocide in the Balkans.

6. Those waiting for the final act, the _____ of big-money television quiz shows, may soon get to say, "I told you so."

7. Are you an expert in Renaissance art or a(n) _____ of Florentine painters?

8. A(n) _____ explanation of new tax laws is probably all that is possible from Jim, who has just begun to read the enormous IRS volumes.

9. In years just before the Civil War, Abraham Lincoln's
_____ grew to include the notion that "all men are
created equal."

10. When Bobby Joe accused Leonard of _____, the
moneylender said, "If you don't wanna pay 100 percent
interest, get cash someplace else."

ANSWERS: 1. gaucherie, 2. oblique, 3. soupçon, 4. bourgeois,
5. heinous, 6. denouement, 7. connoisseur, 8. inchoate,
9. Weltanschauung, 10. usury

Key Terms: Dabbling in Science

If you're a *Star Trek* fan, you probably know about quarks, black holes, and the space-time continuum—even Cyborgs and dilithium crystals. Strangely enough, films and television contribute much to our science and math vocabularies through such varied fare as *Close Encounters of the Third Kind, Cosmos, War of the Worlds, Star Wars, The X-Files, Nova,* and *Contact.*

But there's more. It's a good idea to master the terms that pepper publications and conversations about science. Leaf through *Scientific American* or *Omni* when you loiter at the corner magazine kiosk. And don't toss aside your well-worn copy of the *New York Times* until you've perused the science articles as well. In seeking out bold new terms for your science list, remember to concentrate not only on trendy fields such as biogenetics, but also on the basic foundations such as physics, biology, chemistry, and mathematics. Here's a good introductory list that covers several fields of scientific interest. Can you adopt and use some of these terms in your daily conversations at work or social gatherings?

- **apogee** (the peak, summit, or highest point, particularly used to describe the greatest arc of a rocket): *Captain Flash Gordon's spacecraft reached its <u>apogee</u> at 0935 hours this morning before returning to the inhospitable atmosphere of Mars.*

- **black hole** (a collapsed star or mass in the universe that is dense enough to trap light): *Einstein's Relativity Theory, the classic $E=mc^2$ formula, explains why <u>black holes</u> gobble up light rays and can only be "seen" by their radiation patterns.*

- **BTU** (British Thermal Unit, a measure of heat): *John's electric socks gave off so many <u>BTUs</u> that he received a nasty burn on three of his toes.*

- **chromosomes** (threadlike linear strands of DNA and associated proteins in the nucleus of cells that carry hereditary information): *Humans and chimpanzees have similar distributions of <u>chromosomes</u>, the building blocks of human cells.*

- **clone** (an exact genetic reproduction drawn from the DNA of a living organism): The celebrated case of Dolly the sheep was the most widely reported of many such forays into reproductive science. *At the dawn of the millennium, Tetra, a rhesus monkey, became the first two-legged <u>clone</u> in history.*

- **creationism** (the theory that the Old Testament is an accurate record of human history, beginning with Adam, Eve, and a talking snake): *Matilda's parents sued the school district when Mr. Miller, the biology teacher, refused to present both scientific and <u>creationist</u> accounts of the beginnings of human life.*

- **decibels** (a measure of noise levels): *When Billy's garage band reached an extraordinarily high <u>decibel</u> level,* *blowing out the windows in Mrs. Ferguson's greenhouse, Dad pulled the plug.*

- **dormant** (inactive, but still alive, from the Latin word for *sleep*): The term *dormant* is often used by physicians or biologists. *Some people think that smallpox, instead of having been conquered by a worldwide vaccination effort, is merely <u>dormant</u>.*

- **entomology** (the study of bugs): Not to be confused with *etymology,* the study of word origins. *A team of <u>entomologists</u> from Texas Christian University discovered a living insect that most thought had become extinct in the Neolithic Era.*

- **eugenics** (a word combining the Greek prefix *eu* [good] and the Latin root *gen* [birth]): *Eugenics is the science of creating a superior breed or strain through genetic engineering. In the movie* The Boys from Brazil, *corrupt scientists use <u>eugenics</u> to create a master race of youthful Nazis.*

- **extraterrestrial** (a being from beyond the Earth): *The movie* Close Encounters of the Third Kind *ends with Richard Dreyfuss boarding a spaceship among <u>extraterrestrial</u> beings who want to take him to a distant world.*

- **hologram** (a three-dimensional laser-generated image, such as the early Obi-Wan-Kenobe sequences from the *Star Wars* series): *The audience thought Sting was appearing live at the Oscars, but it was only a sophisticated <u>hologram</u> projected from backstage.*

- **relativity** ($E=mc^2$, Albert Einstein's mathematical description of the laws of energy that drive the physical universe): *The Theory of <u>Relativity</u> explains that space* *and time are curved, meaning that many of the time-travel plots of science fiction are theoretically possible.*

Quiz: Weird Science

As in high school science class, the answers are always multiple choice. Tell the truth. Did you always mark C when you didn't know what you were doing? In the exercise below, identify the correct meaning of the science term at the left, and don't mark all C's.

1. **entomology**
   a. the study of genes
   b. the study of insects
   c. the study of word origins
   d. the study of skin disorders

2. **extraterrestrial**
   a. beyond the bounds of science
   b. outside the city limits
   c. a foreign body
   d. beyond the Earth

3. **creationism**
   a. the theory that the biblical Genesis is historically accurate
   b. the theory that the clergy is divinely inspired
   c. the theory that evolution is a conspiracy
   d. the theory proposed by Albert Einstein

4. **clone**
   a. a genetic duplicate of another being or animal
   b. a copy of the same book
   c. two people who want to be the same
   d. the weakest link in a biological series

5. **chromosomes**
   a. the genetic building blocks of living organisms
   b. multicolored prints
   c. chemicals that influence certain behaviors
   d. the metal trim strips for 1950s American cars

6. **dormant**
   a. something to wipe your feet on
   b. forever asleep
   c. refusing to answer questions
   d. asleep but alive

7. **eugenics**
   a. genetic engineering aimed at producing superior beings
   b. a theory used to study chromosomes in humans
   c. the study of life
   d. the map of DNA in human beings

8. **hologram**
   a. having six sides
   b. a laser-generated three-dimensional image
   c. a graphic representation of the movement of the stars
   d. a very loud noise

9. **decibels**
   a. units to measure sound waves
   b. units to measure sound and noise
   c. units to measure the distance between two points
   d. the highest points in a matrix

10. **apogee**
    a. a summit
    b. the highest point in an arc
    c. where two points meet
    d. close to the ground

ANSWERS: 1. b, 2. d, 3. a, 4. a, 5. a, 6. d, 7. a, 8. b, 9. b, 10. b

Tip of the Day

Brain researchers suggest that our nightmares and dreams are part of a nightly "garage sale" of the mind. During sleep, the brain sorts through the day's impressions, deciding what to discard and what to save. If you want a larger vocabulary, you need to put a "Keep This" sign on your daily cache of new words. Otherwise, when you wake up tomorrow, *connoisseur, apogee,* and *contiguous* will be out on the street corner waiting for the trash collector.

There are several ways to put a "hold" on new words before you hit the sack. First, try to visualize each one. See if you can make *controversy* or *bourgeois* scroll up on the visual screen in your mind's eye. If you can visualize a *neologism,* "a newly coined word or phrase," you are halfway to making it your own. Second, look for mnemonic clues (remember Day 1) in the word itself. Are there some students in your *dorm* who are *dormant* (inactive but still alive)? Third, practice the new words, either by writing them, making and reviewing index cards, or using them in speech or phone conversations. "Hello, I am a *connoisseur* of anchovy pizzas. I hope you're not *averse* to delivering to a sixth-floor walk-up."

With a little practice, you will greet each morning with a larger store of new words.

Like any task, vocabulary building is hard work. At the halfway point of your study, take a moment to review your work. I hope you will find yourself more confident with language and armed with a powerful hoard of useful words.

Tomorrow begins the second half of your ten-day course. In the next lesson, you'll go back home for lessons from Mom. You'll also look at some Greek prefixes that have inspired hundreds of valuable English words. Finally (but not exclusively), you'll look at key terms from the arts and humanities—terms that can help you talk about literature, painting, sculpture, philosophy, and ethics.

Day 6

"I Can't Play That Song—My Instrument Is *Baroque*"

Welcome to the sixth day, famous in Western mythology as a Day of Hard Work (but you're going to make it fun). Roll up your sleeves. First, you'll tackle a hefty section of key terms from the Arts and Humanities. Then there's a good look at Greek-based prefixes, followed by more advice from Mom. Finally, the tip of the day will send you toward Day 7 with some fresh ideas about improving your lexicon.

Key Terms: The Arts and Humanities

Literary and artistic terms are important not only for discussions of plays, novels, and paintings, but also because these words broaden your knowledge and appear in all types of contexts—not just in the arts but in the everyday world as well. For instance, even though *irony* (the use of words to convey the opposite of their literal meaning) is a term derived from Greek drama, you're likely to encounter it during an ordinary day: "Hey, Chuck, don't you think it's *ironic* that the boss is e-mailing his cost-cutting ideas from a five-star hotel in Bali?"

Here's a list of words from the study of literature, the arts, and humanities. As I said, many of the terms have applications in the world at large. Some, like *deconstruction* and *paradox* (definitions to follow shortly), may surface in lively conversations and insightful correspondence. Watch for these key terms in your daily reading and put them to use whenever possible.

- **baroque** (ornate, flowery, or frilly): *The Baroque era, characterized by ornate clothes and interior designs, began around 1600 in Italy, but it's also alive and well today in Las Vegas.*

- **deconstruction** (a literary theory that says a work's true message and meaning cannot be fixed, due to the slippery nature of language): *Deconstruction, imported from France, encourages readers and critics to stop looking for a book's single, unified meaning.*

- **elegiac** (expressing sorrow, mournful): *The poet composed an elegiac work following the death of his friend.*

- **epilogue** (final speech, summary, conclusion): *The author wrote an epilogue at the end of the book to tell readers what would happen to the main character ten years later.*

- **euphemism** (an indirect or vague term substituted for one considered harsh, taboo, or blunt): *Peggy's use of the euphemism "golden agers" began to grate on the older folks.*

- **foil** (a character whose actions and values make the hero seem better): *In* The Rockford Files, *the small-time con man Angel is a bumbling <u>foil</u>, a character who makes Jim Rockford look pretty decent.*

- **foreshadowing** (a subtle clue to upcoming action): *If one of the cowboys in a John Wayne movie draws aces and eights in a poker game, this bit of <u>foreshadowing</u> means that Nevada Bob will take a bullet before the film's conclusion.*

- **genre** (an artistic category like poetry, short story, or drama; genre describes a grouping in cinema, literature, or the arts, such as *gothic* novels or *impressionist* paintings): *Clint Eastwood actually got his start in a film <u>genre</u> known as the Spaghetti Western.*

- **hubris** (pride, inflated ego): In literature, *hubris* is often the tragic flaw of the hero. In the office, a boss with hubris often makes employees disgruntled. In the gym, it's a fifty-year-old who says, "Put some more weight on my leg-lift machine." *This aging quarterback should have retired last year, but his <u>hubris</u> forced him to play one last disastrous season.*

- **impressionist** (describes a work of art that, like Van Gogh's *Sunflowers,* is not a realistic copy of nature, but a personal view filtered through the artist's imagination, one that communicates a mood): *Van Gogh's vivid use of colors and short brush strokes were characteristic of the <u>impressionist</u> painters of the late nineteenth century.*

- **narrative** (a story): *In addition to narratives in art, music, or literature, the long, pointless story in Joe's business report is a <u>narrative</u>.*

- **oxymoron** (a two-word phrase containing contradictory or incongruous ideas): Here are some oxymorons taken from *Crazy English* by Richard Lederer: *mobile home, constructive criticism, recorded live, working vacation, original copy, death benefit, and elevated subway. In the Reagan administration, a budget deficit was known by the <u>oxymoron</u> "negative surplus."*

- **paean** (a song of victory): *The rock group Queen's song "We Are the Champions" is a <u>paean</u> often played by the winning team's band at high school and college ball games.*

- **paradox** (an apparent contradiction that somehow holds a truth): *A great <u>paradox</u> in forestry is the critical need for an occasional fire to strengthen the resistance of surviving trees.*

- **parody** (a humorous imitation of an event or a person): Austin Powers *is a clever <u>parody</u> of the James Bond series, imitating not only the plots but also the characters from the old 007 series.*

- **poetic license** (subtle exaggerations, changes, or deletions of the truth): *The film* Man on the Moon *is a fairly accurate history of Andy Kaufman's life, but actor Jim Carrey took a certain amount of <u>poetic license</u> in re-creating the comedian's character.*

- **pseudonym** (a pen name, literally "false name"): *When writing books like* The Cat in the Hat, *children's author Ted Geisel used the <u>pseudonym</u> Dr. Seuss.*

- **romantic** (describes works that glorify the human condition, suggesting the heroic nature of ordinary people): *My favorite <u>romantic</u> movie is* It's a Wonderful Life, *starring Jimmy Stewart and Donna Reed, where Jimmy Stewart's character overcomes difficulties and hardships.*

- **soliloquy** (a dramatic speech given as though the character stands alone onstage—as compared to a *monologue,* a long speech offered in the company of others): Shakespeare's Hamlet has the most famous soliloquy in literature: "To be or not to be, that is the question . . ." *In the second act, all the other actors left the stage so Daniel could deliver his <u>soliloquy</u>.*

- **surreal** (eerie, oddly contorted, or an exaggeration of reality): *The unsettling Stanley Kubrick film* A Clockwork Orange *presents <u>surreal</u> visions of society, complete with distorted views of reality.*

Pop Quiz: Your Chance to Sing a Paean

Are you ready to sing a song of victory? Good. Here's a chance to test your word-sleuthing abilities against a new set of terms, selections from the arts and humanities key terms. I don't think it's *hubristic* for you to believe you'll do well on this exercise.

1. Detective fiction, like the *Perry Mason* series, is a popular literary _____, a category that often outsells even romance novels.

2. Monet, Manet, and Degas are painters of the _____ school, characterized by an emphasis on imagination and mood.

3. I could tell by the _____ in the opening scene of the mystery play that the butler did it.

4. Phyllis rarely uses taboo words like "toilet," "dead person," and "addiction." She prefers to speak in _____, carefully whitewashed terms like "powder room," "dearly departed," and "chemical dependence."

5. The teacher asked the class members to write a(n) _____ about their favorite family vacations.

6. The high school band played a(n) _____ after the team won the homecoming game.

7. The television show *Married . . . with Children* is a(n) _____ of middle-class American values, poking fun at the sitcoms in the 1950s and 1960s.

8. "It's a _____," said Dr. Goulet, noting ironically that the French, despite consuming foods high in fats, have low rates of heart disease.

9. Isn't "loyal opposition" a(n) _____? After all, if these people were loyal, they'd be friends, not opponents.

10. The boring seminar leader gave a lengthy _____, talking to himself at the microphone, while the audience fell asleep.

11. In a famous _____ scene written by Franz Kafka, a young man, Gregor Samsa, awakens one morning to find himself absurdly transformed into a giant insect.

12. In a great number of movies—*Twins, Romancing the Stone, Tin Men*—Danny DeVito plays the _____, a character whose faults make the leading man seem more noble and engaging.

13. In the Renaissance city of Florence, the _____ style included elaborate gold-leaf furnishings and ornate, intricately patterned decorations.

14. The director decided to provide an _____ at the end of the play to summarize what had occurred between the characters.

ANSWERS: 1. genre, 2. impressionist, 3. foreshadowing, 4. euphemisms, 5. narrative, 6. paean, 7. parody, 8. paradox, 9. oxymoron, 10. soliloquy, 11. surreal, 12. foil, 13. Baroque, 14. epilogue

Key Prefixes from Greek: Does My Winnebago Make Me *Peripatetic*?

In the previous chapter, you utilized some important Latin prefixes. Now we'll return to the Greeks. As you review the sample words, see if they remind you of any other words you use in everyday speech that seem to be formed similarly from prefixes like *an-* or *neo-*.

Prefix	Meaning	Example
a-	without, not	*athiest* (without belief, one who denies the existence of God)
		amoral (not moral, corrupt, depraved, valueless)
		atypical (abnormal, irregular, nonconforming)
amphi-	both, both sides	*amphitheater* (arena with seating on both sides)
(Latin, ambi-)		*ambient* (surrounding completely—on both sides)
		ambiguous (vague, unclear—having more than one explanation)
an-	without, not	*anarchy* (without law, revolution, mob rule)
		anomaly (exception, deviation, irregularity—not the norm)
		anemic (weak, sickly, pale; without adequate blood)
apo-	off, away	*apocrypha* (religious works hidden away, rejected—not acceptable for the canon)
		apoplexy (a stroke, a seizure, one that carries away a victim)
		apostate (one who abandons religion, one who walks away)

Prefix	Meaning	Example
e-, ec-, ex-	out of, outside	*evoke* (call forth, summon)
		excise (cut away from)
		ectopic (medical—occurring outside its usual place)
ep-, epi-	on, upon	*epigram* (a short poem or saying on a single thought or observation, expressed with wit)
		epitaph (memorial, eulogy, often an inscription upon a grave)
		epigenous (developing or growing on an upper surface, as fungi on leaves)
neo-	new	*neonatal* (newly born, premature)
		neoplasm (new growth, tumor, abnormal tissue)
		neophyte (new member, initiate, novice)
para-	beside, beyond	*paraphernalia* (stuff, gear, equipment beyond the essential)
		paraphrase (summarize, restate, translate—a version beyond the original)
		paranoia (fear, anxiety, distrust—to be "beside oneself" with anguish)
peri-	around	*periphery* (boundary, border, outside area)
		periphrastic (roundabout, wordy, redundant)
		peripatetic (wandering, itinerant, walking around)
syn-, sym-	with, together	*synthesize* (put together, unite, build)
		symbiotic (live together)
		syndetic (a grammatical term meaning connected by a conjunctive)

Pop Quiz, Part 1: "Don't Suffer from *Apoplexy*, Man!"

Fill in the blanks with sample words from the list above. The underlined word in each sentence is your clue.

1. When my friend goes camping, she takes so much unnecessary _____, including extra gear and equipment, it is way <u>beyond</u> the amount required for a two-day trek.

2. Marian's egg was fertilized <u>outside</u> the uterus—in the fallopian tube—causing the doctor to say, "We're dealing with a(n) _____ pregnancy."

3. The Cubs winning the World Series is a deviation from the norm, and <u>not</u> standard; in fact, such an unusual occurrence is a(n) _____.

4. That marvelous inscription chiseled <u>upon</u> Uncle Fred's gravestone—"He Could Make the 7-10 Split"—is an unlikely _____.

5. Julia didn't like being called a(n) _____ even though she chooses <u>not</u> to believe in the existence of God.

6. The rock group loves entertaining fans in a(n) _____ because it has seating around <u>both</u> sides of the stage.

7. The philosopher Aristotle was called _____ because he taught his students while walking <u>around</u> the Lyceum in Athens, often stopping to pick up objects or point out natural phenomena.

8. When Uncle Mortimor found that his children had joined a cult, he had such a fit and got so carried <u>away</u> that Aunt Desiree said with alarm, "Mort's just about had an _____ over this Moonie business!"

9. The _____ unit at the brand-new hospital downtown is well equipped to treat <u>new</u> babies and premature infants.

10. The work team tried to _____ all the new information on Web sites, putting it <u>together</u> in a unified version, because the different booklets and manuals were too confusing.

ANSWERS: 1. paraphernalia, 2. ectopic, 3. anomaly, 4. epitaph, 5. atheist, 6. amphitheater, 7. peripatetic, 8. apoplexy, 9. neonatal, 10. synthesize

Pop Quiz, Part 2: Mix and Match

Match the vocabulary word with its definition. The underlined prefix and word will help you make your choice.

1. <u>ambi</u>dextrous
2. <u>a</u>morphous
3. <u>apo</u>state
4. <u>amphi</u>bious
5. <u>e</u>cydysis
6. <u>epi</u>geal
7. <u>ex</u>orcise
8. <u>para</u>normal
9. <u>para</u>pet
10. <u>peri</u>pteral
11. <u>peri</u>scope

a. standing <u>away</u> from the truth, a disbeliever (usually religious)
b. to drive <u>out</u>, to send <u>outside</u>
c. living or occurring <u>on</u> or near the surface of the ground
d. to shed the <u>outside</u> layer of skin, as in insects
e. a low protective wall or railing <u>beside</u> the edge of a roof or balcony
f. a structure with rows of columns <u>around</u> all sides
g. a growing <u>together</u> of bones
h. happening <u>together</u>, at the same time
i. working <u>together</u> to increase effectiveness
j. using <u>both</u> hands
k. an instrument for looking <u>around</u> a 360-degree area

12. s<u>y</u>mphysis l. <u>without</u> form, like warm Jell-O
13. s<u>y</u>nchronized m. <u>beyond</u> the usual, defying the laws of nature and physics
14. s<u>y</u>nergism n. equally capable in <u>both</u> places, land or water

ANSWERS: 1. j, 2. l, 3. a, 4. n, 5. d, 6. c, 7. b, 8. m, 9. e, 10. f, 11. k, 12. g, 13. h, 14. i

Lessons from Mom: Family Comes First

I learned at a young age that family comes before anything or anyone else. When I was six, my dad built a garage in the backyard. While the project was underway, he jury-rigged a lean-to structure against an old cherry tree, and it became the neighborhood fort. The building had two stories, a lookout tower, several secret passageways, and lots of little openings to support rifle fire and cannon placements.

Fort Nash was so cool that everyone wanted to play there, even my sister and her friends. That's when the trouble began. My sister was not only too young; she kept dragging doll furniture and other distinctly nonmilitary stuff into the fort. One day, after I'd cleared Fort Nash of these irregular troops to make room for my own company, General Mom showed up. She made her position pretty clear: "Family comes first."

That was the first of many, many days when Mom stressed the importance of family. When I wanted to take the bus downtown to a cowboy movie, she usually said, "Take your sister along." When I was older, Mom volunteered me to shovel coal for Grandma Mary, pull weeds for Aunt Pauline, and paint woodwork for Uncle Paul. As Mom so often said, "Family comes first."

In the course of learning to appreciate my relatives—and

I'm glad Mom insisted—I also experienced the series of complex relationships that hold families together. Everyone has a role, some more important than others. Cousins, nephews, grandparents, aunts, and uncles—everybody counts. Later, when I began to study anthropology at college, I found that these complex relationships have names, many of them stemming from the Roman era, when family dynamics must have been equally important. Here, from Anthropology 101, are vocabulary selections to describe that intimate and wonderful dance known as family.

Root	Meaning	Examples
avuncu	uncle	*avuncular* (of or having to do with an uncle)
fil	son or daughter	*filial* (benefiting a son or daughter)
		filiation (the condition or fact of being the child of a certain parent)
frater	brother	*fraternal* (of or relating to brothers)
parent	parent	*in loco parentis* (in the position or place of a parent)
mater, matri	mother	*maternity* (the state of being pregnant or a mother; motherhood)
		maternal (relating to or characteristic of a mother or motherhood)
		matriarch (a woman who rules a family, clan, or tribe)
		matrilineal (tracing ancestral descent through the maternal line)

Root	Meaning	Examples (cont.)
pater, patri	father	*paternity* (the fact or condition of being a father; fatherhood)
		paternal (relating to or characteristic of a father or fatherhood)
		patriarch (a man who rules a family, clan, or tribe)
		patrilineal (tracing ancestral descent through the male line)
		patrimony (an inheritance from a father or ancestor)
sib	sister or brother	*sibling* (one of two or more individuals having one or both parents in common; a brother or sister)
soror	sister	*sorority* (an association or society of women)
		sororal (of, pertaining to, or like a sister)
uxor	wife	*uxorious* (excessively submissive or devoted to one's wife)
		uxoricide (the killing of a wife by her husband)

Now let's take a look at how these familial ties are expressed in the sentences below.

- In several South Sea Island communities, the <u>avuncular</u> relationship between a young boy and his maternal uncle is the most important family tie.

- The new study showed that the <u>filial</u> bond between fathers and children is more important to successful maturity than researchers had earlier predicted.

- In the movie *Forrest Gump*, <u>fraternal</u> ties forged in Vietnam between the title character and his friend Bubba make Forrest seek out Bubba's family after the war.

- At the university, the <u>in loco parentis</u> policy literally means that the college will actively stand "in the place of a parent," offering advice and behavioral guidelines for the incoming freshmen.

- When actress Jodie Foster's <u>maternal</u> instinct kicked in, she put her fast-moving Hollywood career temporarily on hold to have a baby.

- The <u>paternal</u> attitude of Franklin Delano Roosevelt toward American citizens was apparent in the president's famous Fireside Chats, a series of radio broadcasts intended to quiet fears about the Depression and America's difficult economic times.

- Some of their friends think that the intensely competitive <u>sibling</u> rivalry in the Thompson family spurred the remarkable political successes of brothers Doug, Charlie, and Tom.

- My friend asks, "Are there witches in *Harry Potter* books?" I don't know. If not, the witches in *Macbeth* are little more than a <u>sorority</u> of weird women.

Exercise: All in the Family

Match the letter and word in boldface with the appropriate sentence.

a. an **avuncular** manner

b. a **filial** agreement

c. a **fraternal** organization

d. an **in loco parentis** policy

e. **maternal** responsibilities

f. a **paternal** attitude

g. **sibling** rivalry

h. a **sorority** event

1. _____ "The school sent a letter home to parents telling them that the school will take responsibility for their child on the field trip."

2. _____ "Now, dear, as your father, I think I know what's best for you, and a vegan diet is not the answer."

3. _____ "Yo, Susie! I, your older and wiser sister, can beat you at anything, anytime, under any conditions. Let's start with three-point shots!"

4. _____ "Listen to me, I'm your mother! You children will fasten your seatbelts now, or this van will not move from the driveway!"

5. _____ "Babs, I look forward every year to the father-daughter retreat, and I'm glad you've made arrangements to go to Camp Arrowhead with me again this year."

6. _____ "Gentlemen of the club! Please put your hands on your heads and give the official Bullmoose Lodge salute! Mmmmmmooooo!"

7. _____ "The Benevolent Sisters of Phoenix charity auction begins with this lovely impressionist print signed by the artist herself."

8. _____ "As your employer, I want you to be happy at work, and so I'm initiating a series of cookouts and company barbecues to get to know each of you

better—I consider you to be as important to me as my nieces and nephews."

ANSWERS: 1. (d) in loco parentis, 2. (f) paternal, 3. (g) sibling, 4. (e) maternal, 5. (b) filial, 6. (c) fraternal, 7. (h) sorority, 8. (a) avuncular

Tip of the Day

I don't like the word *very*. Occasionally, I'll use it, but I always wish I hadn't. The use of *very* means that an adjective (or adverb) will follow, of course. *Very* can't stand alone. But usually the combination of *very* and a modifier is less forceful that a single precise substitute. For instance, a person who is *very happy* is *ecstatic*. Here are some other replacements; you may even recognize some of these words from previous chapters.

1.	very lazy	*indolent*
2.	very out-of-date	*defunct*
3.	very short-lived	*transitory*
4.	very much shortened	*abridged*
5.	very wise	*sagacious*
6.	very negligent	*remiss*
7.	very uncertain	*dubious*
8.	very aggressive	*pugnacious*
9.	very aware	*cognizant*
10.	very pushy	*bumptious*
11.	very decisive	*emphatic*
12.	very fortunate	*propitious*
13.	very argumentative	*querulous*
14.	very shy	*diffident*
15.	very lively	*vivacious*
16.	very talkative	*loquacious*

There are other reasons not to use *very*. For one thing, it's a word, like *thing* or *get* or *stuff,* that has been emptied of meaning through overuse. The difference between *rich* and *very rich* has become negligible in the twenty-first century. For another, the word *very* can sound affected or contrived, as in "I'm so *very* glad you could attend the play!" But the main reason for avoiding *very* remains clear. You can usually find a more precise word to make your point.

Tomorrow, you will investigate key terms from the courts and legal system, then key terms from French. Also you'll visit ways to become more articulate in your speech and writing using a single, concise verb.

Legal Terms, French Phrases, and -*Ologies*

So far, you've acquired a good foundation in Latin and Greek roots and prefixes. There will be a few more scattered through this chapter, but it's also time to look at words borrowed from the French *n'est-ce pas?* The chapter begins with legal terms and, along the way, you'll look at famous -*ologies,* words suggesting "study" or a "scientific approach." Grab a pencil and a tin cup to rattle on the bars. You're making your first stop at the local jail.

Busted! Key Terms: The Courts and Legal System

I certainly hope you don't have occasion to become too well acquainted with words from the legal system, unless, of course, you're planning on a career in torts and litigation. In the meantime, consider this valuable list. Even if these terms may never be necessary for you in the daily grind, you'll need them to keep your bearings during *The Sopranos* and reruns of *L.A. Law.*

- **accessory** (someone who aids or abets a lawbreaker, either before, during, or after the crime, such as the driver of the getaway car or one who harbors a criminal): *Grant was charged as an <u>accessory</u> to the bank robbery after police found one of the suspects hiding in his basement.*

- **affidavit** (a legal document, a sworn statement recorded before a notary public or an officer of the court): *In a notarized <u>affidavit</u>, Warren Schulman affirmed that he had received a shipment of papayas from Bennie Banducci.*

- **altercation** (a fight or quarrel): *Until the authorities threatened to arrest the battling guests, the <u>altercations</u> on the network's new talk show increased its ratings.*

- **caveat emptor** ("let the buyer beware"): *Linda's father told her, "<u>Caveat emptor</u>" before she went to buy a stereo at a garage sale.*

- **collusion** (illegal communication, a conspiracy, a plot): *In a famous legal case, the major league baseball owners faced charges of <u>collusion</u> over players' salaries, the charges coming from members of the players' association. The owners lost, solidifying the era of free agency in baseball.*

- **embezzlement** (stealing money that's not yours but remains under your control): *Carol Anne, the bookkeeper, faced <u>embezzlement</u> charges after the union reported a shortfall of $655,000.*

- **ex post facto** ("after the fact," guarantees to protect people from retroactive actions by governments or individuals): *If the City Council makes it illegal to paint your house orange one month after you finish the job, they're out of luck. In this country, <u>ex post facto</u> statutes prohibit retroactive penalties and judgments.*

- **extortion** (illegal use of one's official position or powers to obtain property, funds, or patronage): *As president of the company, Ronald <u>extorted</u> money from his clients in order to pay for his expensive tastes.*

- **felony** (a serious crime such as murder or burglary with stiff penalties): *The jury found the defendant guilty of <u>felony</u> hijacking and sentenced him to life in prison.*

- **incarceration** (jail time): *The typical period of <u>incarceration</u> for a first-time car thief is three months.*

- **injunction** (a court order barring a specific event or action): *Molly got a court-ordered <u>injunction</u> forbidding her husband to enter their home.*

- **intestate** (die without a will [see *probate*]): *When Edward died <u>intestate</u>, his bank accounts and property languished in court for years.*

- **manslaughter** (the unlawful killing of one human being without planning it): *The defendant was charged with <u>manslaughter</u> after the authorities couldn't find any evidence that he planned to kill his neighbor.*

- **miscreant** (the offender, although the term is considerably weaker than *perpetrator* or *criminal*): *The teenaged <u>miscreant</u> in the school graffiti case has been handed over to juvenile court for sentencing.*

- **misdemeanor** (a less serious offense than a felony): *Debbie's lawyer told her she was fortunate that police only charged her with a <u>misdemeanor</u> for shoplifting from the convenience store; otherwise she could have been given jail time.*

- **nolo contendere** (a plea of "no contest" by the defendant in a criminal action, legally equivalent to an admission of guilt): *Although David admitted he took his brother's Buick without permission, he pleaded <u>nolo</u>*

contendere in court, convinced that "borrowing" from a family member should not be illegal.

- **perjury** (swearing to a false statement under oath): _Christine faced a perjury charge for lying on the witness stand to save her husband._

- **perpetrator** (the one who commits the crime): _After they were able to identify him on the store's security camera, police arrested the perpetrator for robbing the convenience store._

- **plea bargain** (an arrangement in which a defendant agrees to plead guilty to a lesser charge in order to avoid the possibility of full penalty being awarded in a court trial): _John's lawyer advised his client to accept a plea bargain so he would only serve a year in prison rather than three years._

- **probate** (both the court and the procedure for determining the validity of a will and distributing the assets of the deceased): _When Howard Hughes died and several wills appeared suddenly, the entire problem of heirs and beneficiaries was handed to the probate court._

- **pro bono** (free service, such as legal advice for the poor or elderly, coming from the Latin "for the public good"): _In addition to her career as partner in a successful law firm, Judy does pro bono work for families who can't afford to hire attorneys._

- **subpoena** (a written order to appear in court; comes from the Latin "under penalty"): _People who ignore subpoenas and don't appear in court on the appointed day invite penalties, such as a fine or jail time, from the courts._

Pop Quiz: Here's Your Subpoena

Under threat of penalty for noncompliance, choose among the legal terms below and write the appropriate word in the space provided.

a. accessory
b. affidavit
c. altercation
d. caveat emptor
e. collusion
f. embezzlement
g. ex post facto
h. extortion
i. felony
j. incarceration
k. injunction

l. intestate
m. manslaughter
n. miscreant
o. misdemeanor
p. nolo contendere
q. perjury
r. perpetrator
s. plea bargain
t. probate
u. pro bono
v. subpoena

1. An unintentional but illegal killing is _____.

2. A court order telling you to appear or pay a penalty is a(n) _____.

3. A court or process that settles wills for those who die *intestate* is _____.

4. A false statement under oath is _____.

5. Confinement to jail is _____.

6. Misuse of money you are handling but which is not legally yours is _____.

7. A serious crime with serious penalties, such as *manslaughter,* is a(n) _____.

8. A plea of "no contest" is _____.

9. A court order barring any specific action is a(n) _____.

10. Someone who assists in a crime but does not get directly involved is a(n) _____.

ANSWERS: 1. m, 2. v, 3. t, 4. q, 5. j, 6. f, 7. i, 8. p, 9. k, 10. a

Exercise: Replacing Multiple-Word Verbs

One of the best ways to become more articulate in speech and writing involves the effective use of verbs, the action words of language. Well-structured sentences and expressions depend on clear, concise verbs. And yes, some verbs are better than others. It's especially wise to eliminate or reduce your use of two- and three-word verbs. Why? Precision in language follows the *elegance* principle in science. In physics, for example, a solution is *elegant* when it has the fewest steps or the smallest number of working parts. In language, it's often true that the briefest, shortest phrase is also the clearest. Saying precisely what you mean with the fewest number of words is *elegant;* it's also *succinct.*

Consider how you talk when you're not being precise. You can *do away with* that clause in the contract or *eliminate* it. You can *come out with* a new plan for saving money or *announce* the plan. It's better to use the single word, the concise term. Below is a list of common multiple-word verbs and some appropriate substitutes. Practice them in your own memos, letters, e-mails, and conversations.

1. This is not the time to *take on* a new project. (*initiate, commence, adopt*)

2. Don't *give up* if you believe in a good cause. (*capitulate, surrender, acquiesce*)

3. I can't *give away* the secret sauce recipe, I'm afraid. (*divulge, disclose, reveal*)

4. The Sixers hope to *do in* the Pacers on Saturday night. (*annihilate, defeat, eliminate*)

5. Would you rather *do away with* holiday bonuses this year? (*abolish, cancel, eliminate*)

6. Don't *back down* when your son wants a full-body tattoo. (*accede, retreat, yield*)

7. Okay, Bugsy, *come out with* the whole sordid story. (*disclose, divulge, declare*)

8. The Rams will *come through* despite their tough schedule. (*survive, endure, triumph*)

9. Global warming may *bring about* new weather patterns. (*produce, effect, reveal*)

10. Scandal may *bring down* the current administration. (*overthrow, displace, depose*)

11. I hate to *bring up* the subject, but you owe me money. (*mention, broach, introduce*)

12. Can we *get back* the investment we made in Widgets? (*reclaim, recoup, salvage*)

13. Let's *get together* for chocolate cake and coffee after work. (*convene, assemble, gather*)

14. All of us must *come through* difficulties every day. (*endure, survive, withstand*)

15. Too often money can *come between* friends. (*estrange, alienate, isolate*)

16. At the dinner, don't *let on* that you hate broccoli. (*disclose, reveal, divulge*)

Pop Quiz: Using Concise Verbs

In each of the following sentences, I've garbled the statement with two-word verbs. In the space provided, write a clear, precise word that has the same meaning as the two-word verb. In some of the sentences, you may find that a word listed above is appropriate to fill in the blank.

1. Please *take out* _____ the garbage, Phil.

2. Does the newspaper ever *give out* _____ the names of the victims in these extortion cases?

3. When the customer wanted to *rough up* _____ the sales clerk, the manager agreed to reconsider the return policy on electronic equipment.

4. After the election, the Blodgett team struggled to *work out* _____ a deal with Smithers for tax relief.

5. When your chess partner has the advantage, *give up* _____ a pawn rather than a more valuable piece.

6. From my perspective, the team should not *bring in* _____ new players this late in the season.

7. The weather front *came on* _____ unexpectedly from the east and *worked up* _____ the townsfolk, who were unprepared.

8. Alice, would you *work out* _____ somewhere other than in front of the television?

ANSWERS: 1. remove, 2. reveal, 3. assault, 4. negotiate, 5. relinquish, 6. admit, 7. shifted, agitated, 8. exercise

A Plethora (Big Bunch) of *-Ologies*

In previous chapters, you encountered words like *gynecology* and *anthropology*, terms built on the Greek suffix *-ology*, meaning "study of, science of." The suffix derives from *logos*, originally meaning "word." In science, medicine, and technology—as well as most of the arts and humanities—the form *-ology* is a key to understanding important terms and meanings. Here are some memorable *-ologies*. See if you can match the underlined portion of each word with its meaning. You may notice that some of the words were used in previous chapters. That's okay. It never hurts to brush up on newly learned words and their meanings. In addition, this exercise gives you the opportunity to refresh your memory of Latin and Greek prefixes that you've encountered in each chapter.

1. <u>archae</u>logy	a. causes
2. <u>astro</u>logy	b. the universe
3. <u>bio</u>logy	c. new things (words, in this case)
4. <u>cet</u>ology	d. sounds
5. <u>cosmo</u>logy	e. suffering, disease, feelings
6. <u>etio</u>logy	f. whales
7. <u>genea</u>logy	g. writing
8. <u>grapho</u>logy	h. serums such as blood
9. <u>herpeto</u>logy	i. the body
10. <u>hydro</u>logy	j. crime and punishment
11. <u>neo</u>logy	k. birth, origins
12. <u>neuro</u>logy	l. stars
13. <u>ornitho</u>logy	m. animals
14. <u>patho</u>logy	n. places, physical locations and features
15. <u>peno</u>logy	o. water sources, currents, and trends
16. <u>phono</u>logy	p. life, living organisms
17. <u>physio</u>logy	q. snakes and lizards
18. <u>sero</u>logy	r. nerves
19. <u>topo</u>logy	s. history and artifacts
20. <u>zoo</u>logy	t. birds

ANSWERS: 1. s, 2. l, 3. p, 4. f, 5. b, 6. a, 7. k, 8. g, 9. q, 10. o, 11. c, 12. r, 13. t, 14. e, 15. j, 16. d, 17. i, 18. h, 19. n, 20. m

Exercise: Applying New Information

Often the best word-building technique is awareness. Every new magazine, conversation, and exercise provides an opportunity to put your wordsmithing skills to work. Let's try it. Now that you have encountered a number of new Latin and Greek roots in the -*ology* section, see if you can use these linguistic clues to solve the following word puzzles. The underlined word is your key to completing the missing letters of each word.

1. A psycho _____ has a <u>diseased</u> mind.

2. In the brain, _____ transmitters are chemicals that supply information to the <u>nerves</u> and synapses.

3. The smallest unit of <u>sound</u> that has meaning in any language is called a _____eme.

4. A micro_____ is a miniature representation of the <u>universe</u>, one that seems to follow the same laws and trends, only on a very small scale.

5. When your children are <u>born</u>, they become your pro_____y.

6. A small punctuation mark shaped like a <u>star</u> (*) is called an _____isk.

7. A _____ographical map shows the contours and features of <u>places</u> such as mountains, valleys, and streams.

8. When science fiction novelists place twenty-first-century heroes back in time, their Gore-Tex jackets, digital watches, and contact lenses are considered _____chronistic, underscoring the <u>differences</u> between those who belong in that time and those who don't.

9. An _____opter is one of those crazy-looking flying machines that operate by flapping their wings like a <u>bird</u>.

10. A <u>new</u> member of a group, someone just learning the ropes, is a _____phyte.

ANSWERS: 1. psychopath, 2. neurotransmitters, 3. phoneme, 4. microcosm, 5. progeny, 6. asterisk, 7. topographical, 8. anachronistic, 9. ornithopter, 10. neophyte.

Key Terms: The French Connection

When the French-speaking Normans invaded England in 1066, they changed the English language forever, eventually adding thousands of new words, many of them concerned with fashion, the arts, government, and fine dining. Today, a great many of those words and phrases serve as signs of success, style, and acceptance. It is common to say, for example, that a word such as *steamy* may have two meanings, one of them suggestive. The French phrase *double entendre* captures this duality.

Below are some popular French phrases that will come in handy at a good restaurant, in an important meeting, or with friends.

- **à la carte** (ah lah KART): "from the menu," a main course, priced less, without the side dishes, see opposite, *prix fixe,* below

- **avante-garde** (ah-vant GARD): ahead of the times, fashion-setting, a daring approach

- **bon mot** (bone MOE): a clever remark

- **bon vivant** (bon vee VAWNT): a person who has refined tastes and especially enjoys good food and drink

- **cause célèbre** (CAWZ sah leb): "a celebrated cause," a popular occasion

- **cliché** (klee-SHAY): a trite or overused expression or idea

- **coup de grâce** (koo de GRA): from medieval jousting, "a stroke of mercy," the final blow

- **de rigueur** (day ree GUR): fitting, proper, correct— the way everybody does it

- **élan** (ay LAN): flair, style, class

- **fait accompli** (fay tuh kom PLEE): something completed, an established fact

- **laissez-faire** (lay say FAIR): noninterference in the affairs of others, a hands-off policy

- **malaise** (mah LAZ): a vague feeling of illness or depression

- **mélange** (may LONJ): mixture, combination, *potpourri*

- **nom de plume** (nom duh PLOOM): "name of the quill (feather)," pen name

- **pâtisserie** (pah TEE say REE): a bakery

- **pièce de résistance** (pee yes duh ray zees TONCE): an outstanding accomplishment, creation, or event

- **prix fixe** (prie FEEKS): a menu that sets one price to cover an appetizer, entrée, and dessert, altogether— "fixed price"

- **repartee** (reh par TAY): witty replies, clever responses

- **répondez s'il vous plait** (reh pon DAY see voo PLAY): RSVP, "Please reply"

- **tour de force** (toor deh FORS): a feat of strength or virtuosity

Pop Quiz: Leçon Français

Now it's time to test your memory. In the sentences below choose the correct meaning for the word.

1. Which <u>à la carte</u> items do you plan to order: the baked potato, Caesar salad, or fruit compote?
   a. from the menu, priced separately
   b. Dutch treat
   c. senior portions
   d. without regard for calories

2. Using his sword, David delivered a <u>coup de grâce</u> to his opponent.
   a. final scene
   b. final blow, stroke of mercy
   c. knight's duty
   d. denouement

3. The witty, worldly Niles Crane on the television show *Frasier* is the <u>bon vivant</u> of sitcoms.
   a. fussy, difficult man
   b. one who enjoys the good life
   c. frustrated lover
   d. high-strung, nervous character

4. The <u>cause célèbre</u> of the governor's campaign is the plight of the coastal salmon.
   a. celebrated cause
   b. crooked deal
   c. tax plan
   d. overlooked advantage

5. Cary Grant's <u>élan</u>, with his beautiful clothes and debonair manner, was legendary in Hollywood.
   a. list of beautiful women
   b. sexiness

c. appetite

d. style, class

6. Jay Leno's <u>bon mot</u> about his female guest's facelift
    was repeated on David Letterman's show the following
    night.
    a. insulting remark
    b. clever remark
    c. joke
    d. story about one who enjoys the good life

7. Jackson Pollock and Andy Warhol were painters whose
    <u>avant-garde</u> canvases captivated important New York
    art critics.
    a. colorful
    b. ahead of the time
    c. thick and glossy
    d. expressionist

8. Sorry, Paul. That salad is a <u>mélange</u> of wilted lettuce,
    tired vegetables, and suspicious mayonnaise.
    a. high-calorie dish
    b. floral arrangement
    c. clever disguise
    d. mixture

9. Chuck's election as Grand Poobah was a <u>fait accompli</u>
    as soon as he performed his impressive Drew Carey
    impressions at the Moose Lodge's annual talent show.
    a. accomplished fact
    b. popular cause
    c. sorry event
    d. humorous moment

10. At Hillside High, the principal adopted a <u>laissez-faire</u> policy, by making no moves to punish students with blue spiked hair and body piercing.
   a. leave it alone
   b. immediate expulsion
   c. minimum penalty
   d. witty

11. Joan's winter <u>malaise</u> was worsened by Hal's stories about his two-week vacation in St. Croix.
   a. achiness and fever
   b. vague depression
   c. attitude
   d. self-confidence

12. <u>Répondez s'il vous plait</u> to my party invitation by Friday!
   a. send payment
   b. please reply
   c. make your reservation
   d. bring food

13. The <u>pièce de résistance</u> of Alice's dinner party was her famous Jamocha Almond Fudge Cake.
   a. most embarrassing moment
   b. fitting conclusion
   c. best dessert
   d. ultimate event or creation, best part of the meal

14. The dapper gentleman engaged in a clever <u>repartee</u> with the woman sitting next to him on the plane.
   a. swift, witty series of replies
   b. stroke of mercy
   c. hackneyed phrases
   d. gunfight

15. Please stop at the <u>pâtisserie</u> to pick up some dessert pastries.
    a. bakery
    b. pottery store
    c. grocery store
    d. coffee kiosk

16. The <u>nom de plume</u> of Mary Ann Evans is George Eliot.
    a. stylish attitude
    b. pen name
    c. location in Paris
    d. son

17. *Les Misérables* was an immediate <u>tour de force</u> when Victor Hugo's publisher released the novel.
    a. tower of power
    b. powerful, forceful event
    c. chauvinistic attitude
    d. moneymaker

18. "Dumb as a post" is a well-worn <u>cliché</u>.
    a. small exclusive group
    b. proverb
    c. understatement
    d. overused phrase

19. Filing taxes electronically will soon become <u>de rigueur</u>.
    a. required by law
    b. boring and time-consuming
    c. legal, but discouraged
    d. fitting, proper (the way everyone does it)

20. The restaurant offered a <u>prix fixe</u> Valentine's Day menu with three courses.
    a. total cost
    b. fixed price

c. one specialty

d. more than one choice

ANSWERS: 1. a, 2. b, 3. b, 4. a, 5. d, 6. b, 7. b, 8. d, 9. a, 10. a, 11. b,
12. b, 13. d, 14. a, 15. a, 16. b, 17. b, 18. d, 19. d, 20. b

Tip of the Day

Two of my favorite games are *Perquacky* and *Word Yahtzee*. In these games, you throw dice that have letters, not numbers. While trying to beat the clock, players create as many letter combinations as possible to form English words. Let's say the dice cup spills the letters *m, e, t, n, a, r, h, e*. After moving the cubes around the table, you can make words like *harm, theme, heart, arm, neat, hen, tan*, and so forth. Do you see other possible words? Good.

In Day 1, I suggested these word games as a great method for vocabulary building. If you don't have these board games lying around your house, look in the newspaper or in your thesaurus for a long word with plenty of vowels and consonants—something such as *concatenation*," something connected or linked in a series or chain"; *reconnaissance*, "an inspection or exploration of an area, especially one made to gather military information"; or *prestidigitation*, "sleight of hand." Write *concatenation* at the top of a legal pad and see how many smaller words you can create in three minutes. Now try *reconnaissance* and *prestidigitation*.

Get your family involved. Post a word each day on the refrigerator door or the bathroom mirror. Leave spaces for everyone to write derivative words. At the end of each day count how many new words you were able to devise from each word. Here's another good idea. Sponsor some family challenges. "Whoever finds the most words in *Tennessee Titans* gets to control the TV remote on Super Bowl Sunday."

In Day 8, you'll visit Mom for some homespun ideas on how to learn new words. And, among other exercises and tasks, you'll look at musical terms. Until then, keep those pencils sharp and your eyes wide open for new and interesting words.

Day 8

Numbers, Measures, and Lists

Today there's an *intermezzo* (definition to follow shortly) for people who like Itzhak Perlman, Puccini, and *Pagliacci*. From there, you'll receive visits from the bumbling Mrs. Malaprop, who always confuses words, and from Mom, who wants you to make a list. You'll also encounter terms that count. Finally, I'm offering my two cents' worth in the tip of the day, a warning against clichés. Enjoy!

Key Terms of Note: The Language of Music

If you like the Irish Tenors, the Boston Pops, or Kathleen Battle, spend a few minutes studying the language of music. Admittedly, you won't find any terms like "heavy metal" or "ska" in this section. These are terms that represent the Classical tradition in music, from symphony and opera. The expressions are useful, and you may be surprised how many times you'll have an opportunity to employ music terms in everyday conversations.

- **a cappella:** without accompaniment, voices only
- **aria:** a solo vocal piece with instrumental accompaniment, as in an opera
- **chamber music:** music appropriate for performance in a private room or small concert hall and composed for a small group of instruments, such as a trio or quartet
- **concerto:** a composition for a soloist, like a cellist, and an orchestra
- **crescendo:** a gradual increase in the volume or intensity of sound in a musical passage
- **dissonance:** a harsh sound that causes tension, not harmony
- **encore:** an additional performance in response to the demand of an audience
- **falsetto:** a male singing voice marked by tones above the normal range
- **fortissimo:** a very loud passage, sound, or tone
- **intermezzo:** a brief interlude, often light music, played between serious movements
- **overture:** an instrumental composition intended especially as an introduction to an extended musical work, such as an opera
- **pianissimo:** a passage to be played very softly
- **scherzo:** a lively piece in 3/4 time, often the third movement
- **sonata:** a composition for one or two instruments, with three or four movements of contrasting rhythms
- **symphony:** a complex composition written for an orchestra, often in four movements, with the first a sonata and the others varying in style.

Exercise: Play That Tune

Put away your Puff Daddy tapes and Led Zeppelin CDs for a minute. Let's visit the symphony hall. Yes, your tuxedo looks nice. But one question remains: Can you use your new music vocabulary to describe the evening? Let's see. Find the proper music term identified by the underlined terms. Fill in the blanks with the words above.

1. _____ The conductor steps to the stage, and the musical <u>introduction</u> begins. This introduction features many of the musical motifs that you will hear later.

2. _____ The selection tonight is <u>a composition for a soloist and an orchestra</u>.

3. _____ The first movement begins with a fanfare from the brass section. Written on the players' musical scores is the Italian word meaning "play <u>loudly</u>."

4. _____ It's a modern piece, full of <u>harsh, tension-producing</u> chords that are <u>not harmonic</u>.

5. _____ The soloist is a tenor, and he begins singing in a false, throaty style, well <u>above his normal range</u>.

6. _____ In the meantime, the orchestra plays <u>very softly</u>, just loud enough to accompany the tenor.

7. _____ Gradually the music <u>grows louder</u>.

8. _____ Suddenly, the orchestra stops. The tenor has a short section <u>without accompaniment</u>.

9. _____ Now, as the movement comes to a close, there is a <u>lively, joking</u> movement with several lighthearted flourishes.

10. _____ Now the first movement is done. It's time for a brief musical interlude before the second movement starts.

ANSWERS: 1. overture, 2. concerto, 3. fortissimo, 4. dissonance, 5. falsetto, 6. pianissimo, 7. crescendo, 8. a cappella, 9. scherzo, 10. intermezzo.

"I Love the *Motley* Pattern of Your Tie!"

Yes, it's Mrs. Malaprop speaking, back from Day 5. You'll remember that a malapropism is a mistaken word choice, often a near-miss in pronunciation or meaning. Here are several words easily confused, pairs that could lead to an embarrassing *faux pas*. Use this opportunity to practice learning the differences.

- **affluence / influence:** *Affluence* is "a plentiful supply of material goods, wealth, or riches." *Influence* is "a power indirectly or intangibly affecting a person or course of events." *Mary sent her daughter to an affluent school because it had top-notch teachers and academics. Lynn had a strong influence on her daughter's decision to spend a semester studying in Paris.*

- **amoral / immoral:** *Amoral* means "without ethical standards" or "beyond the reach of moral codes" and can refer to animals or young children. *Immoral* people, like Charles Manson, are actively "evil, capable of wickedness even though they are aware of the differences between right and wrong." *Wild animals are amoral, killing only to survive. But people who slaughter baby harp seals for their fur are wicked and immoral.*

- **apathetic / pathetic:** *Apathetic* means "unconcerned or unresponsive." *Pathetic* means "miserable or pitiful."

The congressional stance on campaign reforms is lamentable and <u>pathetic</u>, while the voting public, in response to congressional corruption, grows more and more <u>apathetic</u> about the electoral process.

- **capricious / capacious:** A *capricious* person is "fickle, whimsical, and changeable." *Capacious* means "roomy." *A fan who attends the games only when the Lions are having a great year is <u>capricious</u>. The Pontiac Superdome, where the Lions play, is <u>capacious</u>. It can hold eighty thousand people.*

- **cavalry / Calvary:** *Cavalry* means "troops trained to fight on horseback or in armored vehicles." *Calvary* is "the location of Christ's Crucifixion." *The <u>cavalry</u> rode across the field to prepare for the battle. The tour group visited <u>Calvary</u> to see where Jesus Christ was crucified.*

- **cursory / cursive:** The word *cursory* means "hasty or casual." *Cursive* is "curved writing," the kind you learned in first grade from the Palmer letter charts. Remember Mrs. Adams telling you how to hold your pencil? *In Stephen King's* The Shawshank Redemption, *Andy Dufresne was able to escape because his guards gave his cell only a <u>cursory</u> inspection now and then and didn't see the escape hole he was digging hidden behind a poster. Little Jenny was having trouble learning how to join certain letters in her <u>cursive</u> writing.*

- **explosion / implosion:** An *explosion* forces gases and solid materials "away from" the center, while an *implosion* drives them "inward" toward the center. *When technicians triggered a series of <u>explosions</u> at the Seattle Kingdome, the charges started an <u>implosion</u>, causing the building to collapse into itself.*

- **fatal / fateful:** *Fateful* events are "significant and meaningful." *Fatal* events cause "death." *The <u>fateful</u> events of December 7, 1941, were <u>fatal</u> for thousands of American sailors at Pearl Harbor.*

- **feckless / reckless:** *Feckless* means "incompetent or worthless." *Reckless* suggests "carelessness." *My Great-Uncle Claude recently made some <u>feckless</u> attempts to repair my lawn mower. But when my uncle drove away in his battered Buick, I became concerned about his <u>reckless</u> manner behind the wheel.*

- **gamble / gambol:** *Gamble* means "take a risk in the hope of gaining an advantage." *Gambol* means "play, frolic, or prance and jump." *Jennifer took a <u>gamble</u> when she decided to switch careers. Kathy watched the family of kittens <u>gamboling</u> with their new toys.*

- **germane / German:** The word *germane* means "relevant or applicable." The word *German* means "a characteristic of Germany, its people, or their language." *For instance, the study of word origins is <u>germane</u> to our work with vocabulary building. Linda wanted to learn how to speak <u>German</u> for her upcoming trip to Munich.*

- **infamous / famous:** People who "have a bad reputation" or are "notorious" are *infamous*. Those who are "well known" are *famous*. *The prosecutor described the defendant as an <u>infamous</u> criminal known for his notorious behavior. Debbie couldn't believe she was standing next to the <u>famous</u> musical artist who had just reached number one on the* Billboard *music chart.*

- **limp / limpid:** *Limp* means "lacking or having lost rigidity, stiffness, or the ability to support itself." *Limpid* means "transparent or crystal clear." Speakers and writers often confuse *limpid* with *limp,* leading to some interesting malapropisms for fading vegetables and weak handshakes. *When Tara returned from vacation, she found her plants hanging <u>limp</u> in their baskets, faded from lack of water. Doug loved swimming in a <u>limpid</u> pool because he could see his feet.*

- **mottled / motley:** *Mottled* means "spotted." *Motley,* on the other hand, means "multicolored or made of diverse elements." *The spotted owl of the Northwest woodlands has a <u>mottled</u> coat. Tina referred to her brother and his friends, with their tie-dyed shirts and rainbow-striped pants as a <u>motley</u> crew.*

- **noisy / noisome:** *Noisy* means "a sound that is loud, unpleasant, unexpected, or undesired." *Noisome* is a word like *fulsome.* It's not nice. *Noisome* means "foul or putrid" and, in particular, "bad-smelling." However, because of the similarities to *noisy,* the word *noisome* often is confused with the idea of "bad-sounding." Not so. That word is *cacophony.* *The office was so <u>noisy</u> that Elaine couldn't concentrate on her proposal. David's <u>noisome</u> odor was distracting to the work crew.*

- **razed / raised:** In some senses, these are opposites. *Raised* means "set up in an upright position." The word *razed,* however, means "demolished or destroyed." *In the Amish and Pennsylvania Dutch communities, it is common for people to gather for the purpose of <u>raising</u> a barn. A fire could quickly <u>raze</u> a new barn if the owners are not careful.*

- **want / wont:** *Want* means "desire greatly, wish for." *Wont* means "customary or usual." *Michael said, "I really <u>want</u> the new mountain bike more than anything else for my birthday." The doctor decided to use the <u>wonted</u> method for eradicating poison ivy.*

Exercise: Word Pairs

For each of the following sentences, circle the right answer, avoiding the lurking danger of a malapropism.

1. Every January, throughout the United States, people gather to *raze/raise* their voices in tribute to the fallen civil rights leader Martin Luther King, Jr.

2. For many months, the *famous/infamous* Jack the Ripper terrorized the back streets of London.

3. An *explosion/implosion* in deep space causes a black hole, a star that collapses into its own center.

4. The *mottled/motley* collection of beggars and thieves that surround the young hero in *Oliver Twist* are at once charming and dangerous.

5. "Your *capricious/capacious* attitude toward school, young man, is going to keep you grounded until you're eighteen!"

6. The setting of the most important dramatic scene in the biblical epic *The Robe* is *cavalry/Calvary.*

7. On one *fatal/fateful* day in 1954, the Supreme Court issued its ruling on *Brown v. Board of Education,* ushering in the civil rights era.

8. On Christmas Eve, my fumble-fingered attempts to assemble Sue Ann's dollhouse proved *feckless/reckless.*

9. Mark Twain made it clear that he believed that school boards, like other mistakes, disasters, and calamities, are *apathetic/pathetic.*

10. Factors *germane/German* to horse-racing enthusiasts are track conditions, training records, and breeding.

11. "I'd like to *gamble/gambol* on you as a new employee, Chuck, but I'm not sure your parole board will let you move to Memphis."

12. The *noisy/noisome* Fourth of July party kept the next-door neighbors awake most of the night.

13. The photographs captured the translucence of the lake, its *limp/limpid* waters shining in the morning sun.

14. In *Do the Right Thing*, Mookie's *affluence/influence* over Sal, the inner-city pizzeria owner, helps to explain why the big Italian maintains his close ties with the young man, even after Mookie throws a garbage can through the storefront window.

15. At best, the girl in the bar gave Elionzo a *cursory/cursive* look, leading him to believe he should have stayed home to do the laundry.

16. The sales department was *want/wont* to use the same strategy for Southern states year after year, involving a strong television campaign followed by a targeted bulk-mail program.

ANSWERS: 1. raise, 2. infamous, 3. implosion, 4. motley, 5. capricious, 6. Calvary, 7. fateful, 8. feckless, 9. pathetic, 10. germane, 11. gamble, 12. noisy, 13. limpid, 14. influence, 15. cursory, 16. wont

Terms That Count: What's with the *Sex* in *Sextet*?

Once again, it's the Greeks and Romans who lent English speakers most of their words for numbers and counting. For example, the <u>millennium</u> is a thousand-year period, and a <u>mile</u> was a march of a thousand paces for a Roman soldier. Both words come from the Latin root *mil-,* meaning "thousand." "Thank you" in modern Italian is "grazie mille" or "a thousand thanks." October (from *octo-*, "eight") was the eighth month on the old Roman calendar, which began with March, and November (from *novem-*, "nine") was the ninth. Even words that don't seem to involve numbers sometimes derive from the numeral roots. Words like *quintessence* ("the fifth element, after earth, air, fire, and water") and *diploma* ("a paper folded double") come from the counting traditions of the Ancients. Below are the common Latin and Greek numeral prefixes.

English	Latin Prefixes	Greek Prefixes
one	uni-	mono-
two	du-, duo-, di-	bi-
three	tri-	tri-
four	quad-, quadri-	tetra-
five	quin-, quint-	penta-
six	sex-	hex-
seven	sept-	hept-
eight	octo-	octa-
nine	novem-, nona-	ennea-
ten	decem-, dec-, decim-	deca-
one hundred	cent-	hect-
one thousand	mil-	kilo-

Pop Quiz: Learning Your Numbers

In each space below, write the numerical word suggested by the underlined vocabulary term.

1. The Unitarians, rejecting the Christian concept of the Trinity, see God not as three beings, but as how many?

_____

2. How many events constitute the Ironman <u>triathlon</u>, a popular Olympic event? _____

3. <u>December</u> was which month (by number) in the early Roman calendar? _____

4. If you visit Palm Springs, you'll see some spry <u>nonagenarians</u> riding around in golf carts and wearing leisure suits. Each is at least how old? _____

5. How many tentacles does an <u>octopus</u> have? _____

6. How many sides will you find on a <u>hexagon</u>? _____

7. Joe Johnson's perfectly preserved 1937 Stutz Bearcat is <u>unique</u>. How many are left in the world? _____

8. If you visit Athens and buy tickets for a <u>tetrology</u> of plays by Sophocles, how many performances will you see? _____

9. How many legs on a <u>centipede</u>? _____

10. Billy's garage band is a <u>sextet</u>. How many musicians are singing "Louie, Louie"? _____

11. The most exhausting track and field event is the <u>Decathlon</u>. How many events does it feature? _____

12. How many pieces of paper will you have if you <u>duplicate</u> one? _____

13. A group called an <u>ennead</u>, like the Supreme Court of the United States, has how many members? _____

14. To <u>decimate</u> is to destroy. Originally *decimate* meant to execute a specific number of men, with the victims chosen by lots. According to the word's history, *decimation* is to kill one of every _____ men.

ANSWERS: 1. one, 2. three, 3. ten, 4. ninety, 5. eight, 6. six, 7. one, 8. four, 9. one hundred, 10. six, 11. ten, 12. two, 13. nine, 14. ten

Exercise: Still Counting

Write the numerical word suggested by the underlined word.

1. Your new pet, Phil the Platypus, is a <u>quadruped</u>. How many feet does Phil have? _____

2. You are appointed to a <u>tribunal</u>. How many chairs should you place at the conference table? _____

3. The first several books of the Old Testament, better known as the Torah, constitute the <u>Pentateuch</u>. How many books are included? _____

4. A sabbatical leave is a <u>septennial</u> event, meaning it can occur once every _____ years.

5. Okay, poetry lovers, how many metric beats in iambic <u>tetrameter</u>? Not a poetry fan? How many heads are on the monstrous <u>tetrahedron</u> that attacks space voyagers in *Alien Outbreak on Starbase Zork*? _____

6. How many columns in a <u>hexastyle</u> newspaper layout? _____

7. How many days will a worshipper need to complete the prayer cycle called a <u>novena</u>? _____

8. Today some college dorms are laid out in quadrant style, with one central kitchen and meeting area and several separate bedrooms. A <u>quadrant</u>-style dorm has how many bedrooms? _____

9. In the metric system, a <u>hectare</u> is a quantity of land equaling 2.471 acres. A hectare has how many divisible parts? _____

10. Uh-oh, call the diaper service. It's <u>septuplets</u>. How many babies were born? _____

11. A popular new endurance race is the 50-kilometer super-marathon. How many meters are in a <u>kilometer</u>?
     _____

12. How many valve replacements constitute a <u>quintuple</u> bypass? _____

13. Certain types of geese are <u>monogamous</u>. How many mates does each have? _____

14. The language of computers is <u>binary</u>. How many numbers exist in binary systems? _____

ANSWERS: 1. four, 2. three, 3. five, 4. seven, 5. four, 6. six, 7. nine, 8. four, 9. one hundred, 10. seven, 11. one thousand, 12. five, 13. one, 14. two

Keep Counting, There's More

Yes, there are other ways to express order and number. Here are additional Greek and Latin prefixes that describe measurements.

Latin/ Greek Prefixes	Meaning	Examples
arch-	first	*archetype* (model, first example)
primo-	first	*primal* (first, original)
ulti-	last	*penulimate* (next to last)
		ultimatum (final statement of terms made by one party to another)
multi-	many	*multifarious* (having great variety, diverse)

Latin/ Greek Prefixes	Meaning	Examples (cont.)
poly-	many	*polynomial* (a math expression with two or more terms, such as 2x + [3 x 2] + 5)
equi-	equal	*equipollent* (equal in power, effectiveness, or significance)
par-	equal	*parity* (equality)
holo-	whole	*holocaust* (whole devastation, complete ruin)
		holograph (a document entirely written by the signer)
nihil-	none / nothing	*nihilism* (believing in nothing)
null-	none / nothing	*nullify* (cancel, invalidate)
omni-	all / complete	*omnipotent* (all powerful)
		omnipresent (present at all times and in all places)
		omniscient (knowing everything)
pan-	all / complete	*pandemonium* (complete chaos)
sat-	enough	*satiety* (filled to satisfaction, enough)
hemi-	half	*hemisphere* (half the globe)
semi-	half	*semidiurnal* (occurring or performed during a half-day)

Exercise: Primo-, Ulti-, Multi-, and More

Fill in the blanks below with the prefix, meaning of the root, or a sample word from the above section. The underlined word or syllable is your clue.

1. The next-to-*last* item in a list is called the pen_____-mate one.

2. How many times will an an<u>null</u>ed event take place? _____

3. A(n) _____demic disease like AIDS covers <u>all</u> the world.

4. A(n) _____conductor is a computer material that conducts electricity as though it were <u>half</u> metal and <u>half</u> insulator.

5. If Little Arnold eats macaroni and cheese until he is <u>sat</u>iated, that means he's (finally) had _____.

6. How many numbers will you find in a <u>polynomial</u> equation? _____

7. A complete an_____ation occurs when something is absolutely destroyed, so that <u>none</u> of it remains intact, as happened at Hiroshima when the United States dropped the atomic bomb.

8. In medieval society, the right of the <u>first</u> child to inherit the parent's wealth and privilege was called the system of _____geniture.

9. For the National Football League, the goal of <u>parity</u> means that each team should have a(n) _____ chance for success.

10. A(n) _____farious issue, like the national debate over abortion rights, has <u>many</u> sides, *many* elements.

11. In ancient Egypt, Pharaoh was _____, an <u>all</u>-powerful ruler with the status of a god.

ANSWERS: 1. penultimate, 2. none, 3. pandemic, 4. semiconductor, 5. enough, 6. many, 7. annihilation, 8. primogeniture, 9. equal, 10. multifarious, 11. omnipotent

Lessons from Mom: Make a List!

I spent most of my young life going back to the house for things I'd forgotten: my lunch, my history book, my gym clothes. It was all rather frustrating. The moment I hit the bus stop, I started wondering what was missing.

Mom, of course, had a solution for me. "Make a list," she said. "Write down everything you need for school and check it off before you go out the door." Sensible, orderly, and practical, Mom is a Virgo.

For several years I resisted. Lists were decidedly uncool. Librarians made lists. Discount shoppers made lists. Grandmothers in sensible shoes made lists. No way, José. But, of course, Mom was right. One day, to my horror, I found myself making out a list on the back of an envelope: gym socks, *Catcher in the Rye,* algebra book, lunch money, comb, cool shades, pencil, and stupid essay.

As usual, Mom knew best. I stopped making excuses and started turning in my work on time. I met my appointments. I showed up for a job interview at the Shop-n-Kart with my résumé, my birth certificate, *and* my Social Security card. It worked. The lesson stuck. Today I'm a shameless list-maker. Whenever I head for the grocery store, I carry a rumpled list with forgettable items like chives, pickled herring, and kumquats. Making a list really works, and I recommend it as a way to keep current with your newly acquired vocabulary words.

Just keep a pad and pencil handy—stuffed in your shirt pocket or crammed into your glove compartment. Consider making a game of it. For instance, try to fill daily categories, such as "Words Good Enough to Eat," "Words with an Attitude," or "Words Ending in X." Use your imagination to build interesting list topics. Here's a sample of creative word list collecting.

Words Good Enough to Eat

Don't forget to add some of these tasty treats to your next dinner party menu.

1. **au gratin:** baked with cheese and crumbs
2. **sake:** rice wine
3. **calzone:** folded pizza
4. **petit four:** small decorated cake
5. **ragout:** spicy meat or fish stew

Words with an Attitude

The next time you are at a party see if any of these words describe the guests.

1. **truculent:** ferocious, savage
2. **belligerent:** hostile, combative
3. **loathsome:** repulsive
4. **supercilious:** snooty
5. **presumptuous:** pushy

Words from Greek Mythology

It's never too late to practice words from Greek mythology.

1. **narcissism:** self-admiration
2. **herculean:** very difficult
3. **bacchanal:** party
4. **Dionysian:** ecstatic or wild
5. **Promethean:** boldly creative, original

Words Meaning "Happy"

How would you order these words, moving from the least to the most happy?

1. **blissful:** extreme happiness, joy
2. **exhilarated:** cheerful
3. **contented:** satisfied with things as they are
4. **gratified:** pleased or satisfied
5. **rapturous:** filled with great joy

Words Ending in X

You would be surprised how many words end in the letter X.

1. **phalanx:** compact military force
2. **crux:** decisive point
3. **phlox:** a kind of four-petaled flower
4. **bollix:** bungle
5. **sphinx:** a figure having the body of a lion and the head of a man, ram, or hawk

Getting Acquainted with New Words from the Lists

Now let's practice. Some of the words you've uncovered in list-making will be useful for your word bank. Fill in the blank with the word that best conveys the contextual meaning of the underlined clue.

1. It was irksome enough that Phyllis's date was <u>bad-tempered</u>, but his overwhelmingly _____ attitude toward the Super Bowl party made everyone wish she'd brought her dog, Bobo, instead.
   a. ecstatic
   b. bacchanalian
   c. contented
   d. truculent

2. Out in the yard, Mom noticed a _____ of young boys moving slowly toward the snow fort, a <u>compact</u> force huddled together for protection from the inevitable counterattack.
   a. phalanx
   b. herculean
   c. supercilious
   d. belligerent

3. When the dessert tray finally came, Sharon decided on a <u>miniature</u> vanilla and pecan *cake* with a decoration resembling a Swiss flag. She soon found that the _____ was delicious.
   a. sake
   b. phlox
   c. petit four
   d. ragout

4. With a raised eyebrow and a _____ glance, the eminently <u>snooty</u> Danielle considered the host's wine selection and sneered.
   a. bollixed
   b. narcissism
   c. loathsome
   d. supercilious

5. "Edmund, if you _____ the Andrewson deal with
   your <u>bungling</u>, you'll be working in the mail room by
   this time next week!"
   a. contented
   b. bollix
   c. gratify
   d. phlox

6. "If you wouldn't be so <u>pushy</u>, you'd get more done on
   this project, Al. In fact, it's quite _____ of you to
   assume that management agrees with your choice of
   Tulsa as the site of the manufacturing plant."
   a. narcissistic
   b. presumptuous
   c. supercilious
   d. truculent

7. Although she always kept a mirror in her purse to
   <u>admire</u> her own appearance, Jamie would never agree
   that her actions qualified as _____.
   a. narcissistic
   b. blissful
   c. rapturous
   d. presumptuousness

8. Monica wanted to _____ her new boss, so she did
   everything possible to <u>please</u> her.
   a. bollix
   b. exhilarate
   c. content
   d. gratify

9. On her first trip to the pizza parlor, Emily ordered a
   _____. While she waited for her order, Emily
   watched the chef take the pizza crust and <u>fold</u> it.

   a. calzone
   b. au gratin
   c. ragout
   d. sake

10. Dennis was ready to undertake the _____ task even though his co-workers told him it would be <u>very difficult</u>.

   a. blissful

   b. herculean

   c. loathsome

   d. bacchanalian

ANSWERS: 1. d, 2. a, 3. c, 4. d, 5. b, 6. b, 7. a, 8. d, 9. a, 10. b

Tip of the Day

Expressing yourself well requires more than a powerful word list. It also means using fresh, interesting, and precise phrases. One enemy of articulate speech is the *idiom,* a worn-out expression or overused phrase, sometimes called a cliché. You'll recognize the tired quality of idiomatic language in phrases like "stiff upper lip," "sadder but wiser," or "apple of her eye." Here are four idioms and replacement words for each.

Idiom	*Replacement Word*
1. happy as a lark	jubilant
2. crazy as a loon	demented
3. lap of luxury	extravagance
4. kiss of death	demise

When you feel yourself pull toward a trite phrase, resist the tide. Instead be simple and direct, but clear. With a little practice—and by listening to your own words as well as those of others—you can learn to eliminate a great many of these worn-out words, making room for clearer, crisper expressions.

Day 9 is just ahead. In this *penultimate* section, you'll continue to learn Latin and Greek roots for clues about word building. Also on the docket is an exercise with key terms from history. Keep reading, listening, and gathering. You've completed eight events in your linguistic *decathlon*. Two to go.

Day 9

Why They Should Serve Merlot at a Symposium

Good morning, wordsmiths. Today you're taking a whirlwind tour of the globe, looking for interesting new terms from other cultures. Of course, those stops include Greece and Rome, sources of so many modern English words. You'll also get a crash course in world government and spend time on a single suffix, the highly productive *-ation*. In fact, that's where you begin.

Key Terms: A Collac*ation* (Collection)

Words that end with *-ation,* a suffix meaning "act or quality of," can add scores of new entries to your lexicon. The English language is filled with them. Here are several.

- **coronation:** ritual crowning of a king or queen
- **culmination:** the end, the result, the climax

- **defenestration:** jumping out a window—or being pushed
- **emancipation:** freedom, deliverance, releasing from bondage
- **exhumation:** removing a body from the earth or grave
- **gentrification:** restoration of deteriorated urban properties, especially in formerly working-class neighborhoods
- **hallucination:** a fantasy or vision
- **indoctrination:** a lesson, an initiation, a primer course in the rules
- **infatuation:** being smitten or captivated, a close cousin to love
- **insubordination:** disobedience and defiance
- **lamentation:** loud remorseful cries, wailing, almost biblical mourning
- **peregrination:** journey or travel from place to place
- **predestination:** a prediction, the belief that fate has been ordered
- **procrastination:** stalling, avoiding duties
- **ramification:** consequence
- **reincarnation:** after death, a return to bodily form
- **stagnation:** idleness, inactivity, sluggishness—nothing's happening
- **trepidation:** fear, anxiety, panic
- **vacillation:** indecision
- **verification:** validation, corroboration, evidence, making it "true"

Exercise: Match the Definition

Your task is to match the *-ation* word with its definition in the sentences below. Check your success at the culmination. Good luck.

1. The Calvinist doctrine that your fate has already been determined, even before your birth, is _____.

2. Great sorrow and sadness, weeping and wailing, the type that hits you when you experience upsetting news is _____.

3. Fear and trembling—concern and anxiety—are also referred to as _____.

4. Walking, riding, flying—constant journeying of any kind—is _____.

5. In a royal family, when the heir next in line receives the crown, the event is a _____.

6. The investment of money to convert a lower- or middle-class community into an upper-class area is _____.

7. Putting off the inevitable unhappy chore is _____.

8. "The end is near." The final event, the end result, or the denouement is also referred to as the _____.

9. An imagined, drug-induced vision is a _____.

10. The immediate _____ of any event, such as tooting your horn in traffic, is the consequence (a black eye).

11. A lack of respect, a disagreeable nature, an unwillingness to obey rules is _____.

12. A lack of movement in your stock portfolio is described as _____.

13. The act of releasing someone from bondage is _____.

14. When someone stamps your parking ticket or validates your testimony, that act is _____.

15. When someone believes that a loved one comes back to life in another form, it is described as _____.

16. When a new member of an organization gets a systematic instruction in the rules, procedures, and goals of the organization, it is referred to as the _____.

17. When someone is newly in love and can think of nothing else, that's _____.

18. In a fire, where the doorways are filled with smoke, sometimes _____ is the best way to leave the room, assuming that the windows are fairly low to the ground.

19. A(n) _____ occurs when a body is removed from the ground for analysis.

20. _____ is indecision, as when you can't decide between the cheesecake and the strawberry torte (take the cheesecake).

ANSWERS: 1. predestination, 2. lamentation, 3. trepidation, 4. peregrination, 5. coronation, 6. gentrification, 7. procrastination, 8. culmination, 9. hallucination, 10. ramification, 11. insubordination, 12. stagnation, 13. emancipation, 14. verification, 15. reincarnation, 16. indoctrination, 17. infatuation, 18. defenestration, 19. exhumation, 20. Vacillation

Quid Nunc? (What now?) Roots *ad Infinitum* (Endlessly)

How are you faring with the Greek and Latin roots? Are you finding them useful in your word-building exercises and wordsmithing? *Vade mecum* (go with me), and you'll tackle another long list. When you're done, you can say, *"Veni, vidi, vici"* ("I came, I saw, I conquered"). For each root below, note the meaning and the sample word.

Latin/ Greek Roots	Meaning	Example
ali	other	*alimony* (money paid to the "other" in divorce)
anima	spirit	*animosity* (an ill spirit, ill will between people)
brev	short	*brevity* (a short duration, a brief time)
carn	flesh	*carnal* (having to do with the body, the flesh)
ced	go	*intercede* (interfere, mediate, go between)
celer	fast	*celerity* (swiftness, speed, rapidity)
cred	believe	*credulous* (believe too readily)
dei	god	*deity* (a divine being, a god)
dic	speak, say	*diction* (choice and use of words in speech or writing)
dom	rule	*dominion* (the exercise of control, sovereignty)
don	give	*condone* (pardon, forgive, accept)
equi	equal	*equivocal* (undecided—seeing both sides as equal)
form	shape	*formative* (pertaining to formation, growth, or development)
frag	break	*fragmentation* (the act or process of breaking into pieces)
gyr	whirl, spin	*gyrate* (twist, spin, whirl)
hydr	water	*hydroponics* (raising plants with their roots in water)
loc	place	*locus* (a place, a locality)
lum	light	*luminous* (bright, full of light, radiant)

Pop Quiz: Fill in the Blank

Fill in the blanks below. In some cases, you supply only the root. In most instances, however, you supply the entire word, one from the sample word list. The underlined word is your clue.

1. Philip used a(n) _____ when he registered at the hotel with a name <u>other</u> than his own.

2. After devouring the cheesecake, Anna left only a <u>broken</u> piece, or _____ment, for her husband to savor.

3. Walt Disney's film portfolio of cartoon movies includes a number of <u>spirited</u> _____ted full-length features like *Aladdin, Fantasia,* and *Lady and the Tramp.*

4. _____ is the soul of wit, says the proverb—a reminder to be <u>short</u> and precise in writing and speaking.

5. Audrey, the always-hungry villain in *Little Shop of Horrors,* is a _____ivorous plant. She prefers to eat human <u>flesh</u>.

6. Wanda is so _____ she'll <u>believe</u> anything you tell her.

7. The irascible Q on *Star Trek* is a _____, a <u>divine</u> being who takes an incarnate form when he makes his unwelcome appearances on Picard's starship.

8. The international journal of bad <u>speech</u> and words, edited by Professor Reinhold Aman, is called *Male _____ta,* a vast collection of curses and insults.

9. The king stood before the peasants and cried, "I have sole _____ over this land and I will <u>rule</u> forever."

10. Big Eddy got his pardon from the governor, but his mother refused to <u>give</u> Eddy her own blessing of forgiveness. She doesn't _____ the use of violence.

11. Be _____ when it comes to saving the environment. Don't accept as <u>equal</u> any opinions that refer to strategies that may pollute the water and air.

12. The Re_____ party wants to <u>reshape</u> American politics.

13. When Elvis Presley first appeared on *The Ed Sullivan Show* in the 1950s, he was instructed not to _____ before the cameras, for fear that his hip-<u>twisting</u> style would corrupt viewers' minds.

14. Rabies, also called _____phobia, is so called because its victims have an abnormal fear of <u>water</u>.

15. With a beautiful backdrop of fading <u>light</u>, the dusky sky was beautiful and mysteriously _____.

16. Have you noticed that payday never approaches with even a hint of <u>swiftness</u>, while tax day always approaches with _____?

ANSWERS: 1. alias, 2. frag, 3. animated, 4. Brevity, 5. carn, 6. credulous, 7. deity, 8. dict, 9. dominion, 10. condone, 11. unequivocal, 12. form, 13. gyrate, 14. hydro, 15. luminous, 16. celerity

Top Ten List: Government Types

An essential element of a well-rounded vocabulary is an understanding of the various forms of government worldwide and throughout history. Following are the major governing types or governing bodies.

- **aristocracy** (government by the nobility, a privileged minority, or the upper class): *In Massachusetts politics, the long-standing dominance by the wealthy Kennedy family has often been called an example of American aristocracy.*

- **democracy** (government of, by, and for the people): *Because the United States is a democracy, all citizens, except those disqualified for criminal acts, have the right (and obligation) to vote.*

- **despotism** (government or political system in which the ruler exercises absolute control): *Cuba's form of government is called despotism because the country is ruled by a dictator who tells citizens how to live.*

- **gerontocracy** (a governing group of elders): *The retirement community favors a gerontocracy because all the residents are over sixty.*

- **monarchy** (rule by one person): *The history class learned that, in the Elizabethan era, England was ruled by a monarchy, with Queen Elizabeth making most decisions, often to the great frustration of Parliament.*

- **theocracy** (rule by a dominating religion, with the holy ones representing God on earth): *In Iran and other historically Muslim states the governing principle, in which the rulers believe in Allah, is theocracy.*

- **timocracy** (occurs when only citizens possessing property can vote, hold an office, and govern): *The early American colonies qualified as timocracies.*

- **totalitarianism** (absolute dictatorship with no checks and balances): *Hitler and Stalin led totalitarian governments by keeping their respective countries under strict rule.*

Exercise: Government 101

Let's test your knowledge of historic and world government. Match the type of government with its definition.

1. In George Orwell's *1984*, the fact that Big Brother was watching everyone, controlling every move, action, and thought, meant that the state was ruled by _____.

2. Rule by the clerics, the holy ones, representing God's edicts and judgment, is a(n) _____.

3. Government of the people, by the people, and for the people is a(n) _____.

ANSWERS: 1. totalitarianism, 2. theocracy, 3. democracy

Terms from Around the World

The English language is not only influenced by French; we've assimilated terms from several different languages. Each of the following comes from one of seven different languages. See how many you recognize.

Italian

- **al dente:** cooked enough to be firm but not soft
- **al fresco:** in the open air
- **trattoria:** restaurant

Japanese

- **bonsai:** dwarfed and sculpted tree or plant
- **origami:** flower arranging
- **sayonara:** goodbye

Chinese

- **pidgin:** a simplified combination of two or more languages spoken for ease of communication
- **tofu:** a molded fermented soy cake with a custardlike consistency
- **typhoon:** a hurricane at sea

Irish Gaelic

- **banshee:** female spirit warning of death
- **brogue:** a heavy Irish accent
- **blarney:** smooth talk, quick wit, not overly burdened with a concern for facts

Russian

- **intellgentsia:** the intellectual class—philosophers, teachers, deep thinkers
- **mammoth:** an extinct elephant—also generalized to mean "huge"
- **steppe:** a plain, a grassland, a prairie—often a high meadow

Spanish

- **bodega:** wine shop
- **mesa:** flat-topped mountain, a "table" mountain with steep sides
- **desperado:** a bad guy, outlaw

German

- **angst:** fear and anxiety
- **gasthaus:** guest house
- **gemütlichkeit:** comfort, courtesy

An Approach to Foreign Terms

Well, that was a rapid world tour. Did you learn some new words? To help these words find a permanent place in your word bank, let's see how well you retain their meanings. Match the term on the left with its corresponding meaning on the right.

1.	desperado	a.	goodbye
2.	banshee	b.	the bad guy
3.	blarney	c.	huge, immense, historic
4.	typhoon	d.	female spirit warning of death
5.	sayonara	e.	smooth talk, quick wit
6.	mammoth	f.	cooked to firmness
7.	al dente	g.	the Gaelic speech style of Victor McLaglen in *The Quiet Man*
8.	angst	h.	it's bean curd, but so good for you
9.	trattoria	i.	order ravioli, lasagna, cannelloni, and a hearty Chianti here
10.	tofu	j.	a cyclone at sea
11.	pidgin	k.	a combination of two (or more) languages
12.	gasthaus	l.	fear and anxiety
13.	bonsai	m.	guest house
14.	mesa	n.	a dwarfed tree, shaped and sculpted by an artisan
15.	brogue	o.	high plateau

ANSWERS: 1. b, 2. d, 3. e, 4. j, 5. a, 6. c, 7. f, 8. l, 9. i, 10. h, 11. k, 12. m, 13. n, 14. o, 15. g

Key Terms from History:
"Hey, You're Losing Your *Bombast*!"

One of the best ways to remember a word is to learn the story behind the word's origins. Some words come from significant events or from the names of important people. Other words have more *pedestrian* (common), but interesting, histories. Below are several terms with odd or intriguing pasts, many of them contributed originally by Charles Earle Funk, in *Thereby Hangs a Tale*, or Willard Funk, in *Word Origins and Their Romantic Stories*.

- **amazon** (a tall, vigorous, strong-willed woman): Homer wrote of the Amazons, impressive women warriors who once invaded Greece. The women met with groups of men once a year, but kept only the female babies, sending the boys to neighboring tribes. *Robbie refers to his wife as an <u>amazon</u> because, although she isn't particularly tall, she always stands up for herself and states her beliefs.*

- **amortize** (liquidate a debt by making a schedule of payments): The root of *amortize* is *mort,* meaning "death." In medieval days, to *amortize* was to kill or destroy anything living. But with the increasing ownership of land by peasants, the term gradually acquired a special legal sense, the gradual "killing" of a real estate debt through payments. *Susan wanted to <u>amortize</u> her credit card debt by making two payments a month.*

- **berserk** (crazed or uncontrollable): In Norse mythology, the berserkers were part of a famous family of warriors—a father and twelve belligerent sons—who wore bear-shirts into battle. *Lucy went <u>berserk</u>,* *screaming and waving her arms around, when she came from the grocery store and saw that someone had vandalized her car.*

- **bombast** (pretentious, wordy speech or writing): Is bombast just stuffing? Yes. In the medieval world, a knight's armor was cold, hard, and uncomfortable. Knights put cotton batting called bombast under the steel to ease the discomfort. *Ally delivered a <u>bombastic</u> speech that went on for twenty minutes.*

- **chivalry** (politeness; courtesy; use of good manners, particularly by men toward women): In the era of the Normans in France, a *chevalier* was a mounted warrior. Chivalry came to be known as the code of the horse-borne knights, a lifestyle celebrated in *Camelot. Linda told her mother that <u>chivalry</u> was dead because her last date was impolite.*

- **colossal** (huge, enormous, and often imposing): The Colossus of Rhodes, one of the Seven Wonders of the Ancient World, was a statue of Apollo standing 105 feet high in the ancient Greek seaport. Later, the huge amphitheater in Rome came to be known as the Colosseum, a reference to the theater's enormous proportions. *Audrey made a <u>colossal</u> mistake when she gave her boss the wrong report to deliver at the conference.*

- **curmudgeon** (a bad-tempered person, usually elderly): The word probably comes from a combination of the French *coeur,* "heart," and *méchant,* "evil." *Lisa's father was always grumpy, complaining about everything, with never a kind word to anyone. All the kids called him a <u>curmudgeon</u>.*

- **diplomat** (an ambassador, an official governmental representative, often carrying documents or information to others): A *diploma,* we know, is a paper folded in two. A diplomat traveling from Ancient Rome usually carried two tablets or one folded sheet, signed and sealed as evidence of the courier's authority. *The diplomat from Italy was called to attend the important international meeting so that his country's interests would be well represented.*

- **gospel** (holy writing): When the Church sent Latin-speaking missionaries throughout the world, they carried the *evangelium,* "good news." On reaching Anglo-Saxon soil, the missionaries learned the English equivalent for *evangelium.* It was *god* ("good") *spel* ("tale, story"), later becoming *gospel. Gospel music is indeed "good news" in Radio City, with religious albums selling record numbers throughout the country.*

- **gregarious** (sociable, friendly): Think of a herd of sheep. The Latin root *greg-* means "herd" or "crowd." When Romans saw Caesar's military legions gathering like a flock of grazing animals, they applied the term *gregarious,* meaning "like a herd." Today, gregarious people like to spend time with others. *Susie loved her sister's new boyfriend because he was so gregarious and always invited her to join them at parties and special events.*

- **hector** (to badger or bully people): In Homer's *Iliad,* Hector was the Trojan champion, a man of limitless courage. The name *Hector,* however, fell on hard times later. In the 1600s, the streets of London were sometimes filled with bands of roving troublemakers. With great irony, the people whose windows they smashed and carts they overturned called them *Hectors.*

*When the Philadelphia Sports Nut decided to <u>hector</u>
Shaquille O'Neal during a basketball game, the Big Man
stopped the badgering with one withering look.*

- **knickers** (short pants): This style was popularized by
  the family of Dutch settler Harmen Knickerbocker, an
  emigrant to Albany, New York, in the years following
  1680. Recent members of New York's professional
  basketball team, the New York Knickerbockers—better
  known as the Knicks—also wear short pants. *When he
  put on his new private school uniform—a white shirt, tie,
  navy blue jacket, and <u>knickers</u>—Angelo was so
  embarrassed that he almost refused to go to school the
  first day.*

- **nepotism** (the hiring or promotion of relatives, often
  without consideration of their credentials): Nepotism
  means "nephew-ism" in the original Greek. According
  to Charles Earl Funk, this brand of political favoritism
  was championed by Rodrigo Borgia, Pope Alexander
  VI, who bestowed wealth, lands, and offices on his
  sons, nephews, and other relatives at the turn of the
  sixteenth century, inspired the word *nepotism* in the
  process. *Over lunch, at the dress company, Gina and
  Clara accused their new boss, Ms. Highbrow, of <u>nepotism</u>
  because she had hired her own two daughters, who didn't
  have any experience in fashion design or marketing.*

- **nostrum** (a cure): During the years of the Great Plague
  in England, when thousands of Londoners died each
  month, street-corner vendors sold "cures" in bottles
  and vials. Several charlatans from the mainland, in
  order to show their learning, printed the Latin word
  nostrum on the bottles. *Nostrum,* however, makes no
  claims. It simply means "our own." It was like writing
  "I made this stuff" on the label. *My grandmother*

concocted this wonderful <u>nostrum</u> to cure chest colds, consisting of peppermint balm, oil of wintergreen, and camphor oil.

- **panorama** (a spectacular view; a wide perspective, often greater than 180 degrees): In the late eighteenth century, artist Robert Barker created a work of art that offered a continuous view. He built a rotunda and painted a 360-degree landscape inside. After climbing a stair, viewers found themselves completely surrounded by scenery. Barker called his technique *panorama,* a word formed from the Greek *pan* ("all") and *-orama* ("view"). *As we stood on the parapet at the top of the Duomo in Milan, we could see the whole city, a <u>panorama</u> of stunning architecture and the rolling hills.*

- **sardonic** (mocking, scornful, or sarcastic): In ancient Greek lore, the island of Sardonis grew a plant so bitter and toxic that anyone eating its buds showed a scornful, ironic face before death. That look came to be known as sardonic. *My father-in-law makes the most <u>sardonic</u> remarks at dinner, and he always ends up hurting someone's feelings.*

- **shibboleth** (a password, a verbal "key" for entry): Shibboleth means "ear of corn" in Hebrew. In a tribal war, the biblical Ephraimites were infiltrating the lands of their neighbors, the Gileadites. At the Jordan River, the Gileadites established a checkpoint. Because the Ephraimites spoke a Hebrew dialect without the "sh" sound, they could not say *shibboleth* correctly, so the Gileadites made it the password. Those who stumbled on the password were executed as spies. *The kids down the street have a secret club and if you don't know the right <u>shibboleth</u>, they won't let you in the door.*

- **symposium** (a conference or convention): "A drink after dinner?" "Thanks, I'd love one." Such an "exchange" in Ancient Greece was called a symposium. The wine came after the meal, when the men (no women were allowed) retired for libations. The word *symposium* comes from a phrase meaning to gather "with a potion." *Mr. MacIntyre said the whole department was going to attend the three-day <u>symposium</u> on Internet marketing. We're so excited because it's being held at the Grand Hyatt in Maui.*

- **tawdry** (showy but gaudy and lacking in taste): In Saxon England, a virtuous young girl named Ethelreda took holy vows. After an exemplary life in the nunnery, she died of a throat disease. Ethelreda, later canonized as St. Audrey, had blamed her disease on her one sin, a girlish obsession with fancy necklaces. On her birthday, October 17, hawkers sold St. Audrey lace in memory of the saint. The "s" was lost in dialect, and eventually cheap, showy embroidery came to be known as *tawdry laces. At the opera last week, I saw a woman with the most <u>tawdry</u> outfit. She wore a huge red velvet cape and gobs of costume jewelry around her neck.*

- **utopian** (an ideal society): In fact, the word means "not a place," taken from the Greek *ou* ("not") and *topos* ("place"). In Greek stories, utopian societies were not real, but imaginary—hence the name. In the sixteenth century, Sir Thomas More published *Utopia,* his fanciful account of an island with the perfect economic, social, and political systems. He said the island was discovered by a friend of the explorer Amerigo Vespucci. *Alexa and Martin dreamed of living in a <u>utopian</u> society, one without drugs and violence.*

Exercise: Don't Get Your *Knickers* in a Twist, but It's a Quiz!

Let's practice these terms with fascinating histories. If you can remember the story behind the term you'll probably recall its meaning as well. For each sentence, fill in the term that fits best by association.

1. Echinacea, lemon, eye of newt, ginseng, cherry cough syrup, and a pinch of coriander is Joe Schwarz's phony _____ for curing the flu.

2. Great-Aunt Agatha's Thanksgiving Day outfit of giant earrings shaped like the Eiffel Tower, a red, white, and blue hat with a picture of Uncle Sam on top, and gold-painted necklaces made of old beer can pop tops could only be described as truly _____.

3. Nobody knew the handsome young man at the barbecue, but he was shaking hands with everyone in the crowd and was certainly the life of the party, with his _____ manner.

4. The restaurant patron asked the waiter to describe the six-foot Garbage Grinder with provolone, feta, roast beef, ham, Swiss, mayonnaise, mustard, bean sprouts, lettuce, tomatoes, onions, peppers, and turkey. The waiter said, "It's _____!"

5. After the mayor hired his cousin as a dogcatcher with an annual salary of $90,000, the staff grew resentful of the politician's _____.

6. When you stand on the rim of the Grand Canyon and look at the stunning view, you're certain to be swept away by the _____.

7. In World War II, American GIs used phrases like "Mickey Mouse" and "Donald Duck" as _____,

reasoning that the Nazi soldiers wouldn't be able to guess them.

8. A series of formal workshops or meetings of an organization such as the Save the Whales Foundation, Mothers Against Drunk Driving, the National Council of Teachers of English, or the California Wine Growers' Association is called a(n) _____.

9. Telemarketers, aggressive panhandlers, guys with squeegees at intersections, phone company recruiters, and certain religious zealots are _____.

10. Some viewers of *Camelot,* quoting the line "the rain shall never fall 'til after sundown, by eight the morning clouds must disappear," call it _____.

11. Saying to someone wearing jeans and sneakers, "I can tell you must really have a skewed view of what constitutes professional dress," is a(n) _____ remark.

12. Ronald in sales went _____ after losing his fourth account this year, throwing his cup of coffee across the room and yanking his phone from the wall.

13. Greta called the obnoxious speeches and stuffed-shirt gobbledygook of many political candidates _____.

14. That new, really tall model in my favorite fashion magazine, with her broad shoulders and powerful arms, looks like a(n) _____.

15. Steve arranged to _____ his debt with monthly payments of $674.45 for thirty years, but having to pay all that interest really killed him.

16. My neighbor was once sweet, but through the years, he's become mean and cranky. I think he's nothing but a(n) _____.

17. The movie's costume designer used incredible detail. The clothing of all the characters, including the _____ the little boys wore, was historically accurate.

18. My sister is going to major in international relations because she wants to be a(n) _____ overseas.

19. Chapters of the Bible—including Matthew, John, Zechariah, Ruth, Isaiah, and Ezekiel—are considered _____.

20. Andrew is the epitome of _____ because he's always opening doors for women, giving up his seat on the bus to the elderly, and letting others step before him in line.

ANSWERS: 1. nostrum, 2. tawdry, 3. gregarious, 4. colossal,
5. nepotism, 6. panorama, 7. shibboleths, 8. symposium,
9. hectors, 10. utopian, 11. sardonic, 12. berserk,
13. bombast, 14. Amazon, 15. amortize, 16. curmudgeon,
17. knickers, 18. diplomat, 19. gospels, 20. chivalry

Tip of the Day

Sometimes an effective way to study a word is to investigate its antonyms, words that mean the opposite. For instance, *flaccid* means "drooping." Antonyms include *rigid* or *stiff*. *Scintillating* means "bright" or "clever." Its opposites include *boring* and *dull*. Remembering these antonyms—and those for other vocabulary selections—is a context skill that makes use of the brain's natural tendency to find contrasts.

In fact, the human mind has systematic programs for both comparing and contrasting, lumping together and separating. When children first learn language, they make mistakes that reveal the process, substituting "hot" for "cold," "in" for "out," "bow-wow" for "kitty-cat." As they do in so many processes of cataloguing, children first lump together words by association (words for household pets), then start marking meaningful distinctions ("birdie," "doggie," "kitty").

Several vocabulary books, Web sites, and word-builder programs take advantage of your natural tendency to define by opposition. One such resource is *The 21ˢᵗ Century Synonym and Antonym Finder* by Barbara Ann Kipfer, edited by the Princeton Language Institute. Another is the Internet, where you can type in the key word *antonym* and scan the many possibilities. Even a good dictionary has an antonym section.

If you're making context cards or just keeping a list in your purse, consider adding antonyms. When you discover that *disgruntled* means "unhappy," also jot down *satisfied,* an antonym. When you find that *pacific* means "peaceful," write down its opposite, the word *violent.* Over time, this method will help you retain each new word—remembering not only the definition, the word associations, and the etymology, but also terms that mean the opposite.

In Day 10, you'll conclude your work with yet more Latin and Greek roots, hear advice from Mom once again, and learn some great new ideas about where to be a word sleuth. Finally, you're going to learn more about food, dining, and cuisine.

Day 10

Be *Tenacious* in Your Pursuit of New Words

In this final day, you'll look at wonderfully delicious words from the world of fine dining, and you'll also hear from Mom about places to acquire new words. But the place you'll start, of course, is the language of the Ancients, beginning with more essential Latin and Greek words.

Key Terms from the Ancients: Your Work Is *Magnificent*

As in Day 9, it is important to learn the meaning of these roots. After reviewing the list, answer the questions below.

Greek/ Latin Roots	Meaning	Example
grad	step	*degrade* (reduce in status or rank)
gress	step	*digress* (step away from the primary topic)
magn	great	*magnanimous* (noble of mind and heart, especially generous in forgiving)

Greek/
Latin

Roots	Meaning	Example (cont.)
med	middle	*medieval* (of the Middle Ages)
migr	wander	*migratory* (on the move, transient, wandering)
mut	change	*mutation* (change, often in a biological sense)
nov	new	*novelty* (the quality of being new)
oper	work	*operose* (involving great labor)
pac	peace	*pacific* (peaceful, calm)
petr	stone	*petroglyph* (a prehistoric drawing or painting on stone)
port	carry	*deport* (carry away from a country, expel)
purg	cleanse	*purge* (to cleanse, to remove undesirable elements)
reg	rule	*regime* (ruling body, governing group)
simul	same	*facsimile* (a copy, such as a fax)
spir	breath, life	*spirometer* (an instrument for measuring the volume of air entering and exiting the lungs)
stell	star	*stellar* (starlike, superior, brilliant, extraordinary)
stig	mark	*stigmatize* (to brand with dishonor, to mark with shame)
tard	slow	*tardy* (late, slow to arrive)
term	end	*terminus* (a boundary or border)
vali	strong	*valiant* (possessing or displaying courage, strength)
ver	true	*veracity* (truth)

Exercise: The Answers Is . . .

Fill in the blanks, sometimes supplying only the root; in other instances, give the entire word from the sample list. Underlined words are your clues.

1. At least by name, the _____ Ocean is the most <u>peaceful</u>.

2. Clarence stood in the <u>middle</u> of the angry workers and tried to _____iate their differences.

3. The musical <u>work</u> of a classical composer in which the lyrics tell a compelling dramatic or comedic story may be considered a(n) _____.

4. Jane found the perfect _____ty to bring to the surprise party—a life-size poster of the guest of honor.

5. Overlooking the Columbia River, etched and painted into <u>stone</u>, is *She Who Watches,* a Native American artifact commonly identified as a(n) _____.

6. In Catholic theology and Dante's descriptions of the afterlife, _____atory is the place of punishment where the guilty <u>purge</u> their sins.

7. Because each of Mary's children had performances or presentations at the <u>same</u> time on Tuesday night, her husband complained, "I can't understand why the school district schedules so many _____taneous events."

8. When a hereditary ruler is too young to take the throne, a _____ent often takes office—a caretaker who <u>rules</u> until the child comes of age.

9. _____mata is a rare phenomenon that leaves a bloodied <u>mark</u> on the palms in sympathy with Christ's wounds.

10. In Steinbeck's *The Grapes of Wrath,* the Joads are _____ant farmers from Oklahoma who <u>move</u> to California in hopes of finding better lives.

11. A fire re_____ant <u>slows</u> the flames.

12. In the middle of her presentation on herbal medications, Sally Sue <u>stepped</u> away from the head table and began to _____, speaking unexpectedly on the shortcomings of the American health care system.

13. The _____ of the route was marked on the map with big letters that indicated the <u>end</u> of the state line.

14. In 1215, at Runnymede, King John of England was forced by the nobles of his kingdom to sign a <u>great</u> bill of rights called the _____ Carta.

15. Matthew was called a(n) _____ant hero for his <u>strong</u>, brave fearlessness during the battle.

16. A _____ performance by singing <u>star</u> Celine Dion helped *Titanic* win the Oscar for Best Musical Score.

17. Every day the science class watched the animals undergo biological <u>changes</u>. The teacher said the _____ takes three weeks.

18. Bags, boxes, folders—anything you can <u>carry</u> onto an airplane—is _____able.

19. Because <u>truth</u> is so important to any relationship, counselors often insist that _____ is the core of a successful marriage.

20. The respiratory specialist used a _____ometer to check the patient's <u>breathing</u> sounds.

ANSWERS: 1. Pacific, 2. med, 3. opera, 4. novel, 5. petroglyph, 6. Purg, 7. simul, 8. reg, 9. Stig, 10. migr, 11. tard, 12. disgress, 13. terminus, 14. Magna, 15. vali, 16. stellar, 17. mutation, 18. port, 19. veracity, 20. spir

A Decalogue: Terms with the Root *Ten*

In Latin, the word *tenere* means "hold." The singer who holds the melody in a group is the *tenor*, especially if it's Pavarotti. *Tennis* is a game where the object is to "hold" the ball within the confines of the court. Here, from the *Reader's Digest Family Word Finder*, are five useful *ten* terms, each with the notion of "holding."

- **lieutenant** (holds power in *lieu* of a superior, such as the captain, king, CEO): *The lieutenant oversaw the combat mission while the captain was detained at a meeting with the president.*

- **tenacious** (a person who holds firm, remaining stubborn and immovable): *Linda was tenacious in her belief that women are equal to men.*

- **tenet** (a belief held solidly—an opinion, a doctrine, or a position): Tenet, by the way, is a palindrome! *The tenets of his religion forbid Doug from opening his business on the Sabbath.*

- **tenure** (position held for a certain number of years, such as a judge's *tenure* on the bench or a professor's tenure at the university): *Miller and Donald gained tenure on the teaching staff after three years of stellar performances.*

- **untenable** (an unreasonable, unsupportable position— an opinion that cannot be defended): *David told his pupil that if he had checked the facts before writing his term paper, he would have found his argument untenable, because the data were more than five years old.*

Those *Ten* Roots Keep Popping Up

Other *ten* words come from the Latin *tendere* meaning "stretch, twist, hold, or extend." Your *tendons* stretch throughout your body. When you're *tense,* the muscles and tendons stretch tightly. Even a *tent* is a structure of fabric stretched over poles. Here are some *ten* words that capture the idea of stretching.

- **contentious** (a person who is always competing, striving against others, stretching to win an argument or an advance): *Peggy's contentious determination to win the debate was evident in the length and fortitude of her rebuttal.*

- **distended** (distorted, twisted, or bulged out—like a *distended* blood vessel): *When police found the abandoned children, their stomachs were distended from malnutrition.*

- **ostentatious** (showy, boastful, stretched out for display before others): *Philip told his wife that her dress was too ostentatious for the dinner party.*

- **pretentious** (people who stretch the truth, creating a false view of themselves): *Critics immediately called Al Gore pretentious after he claimed to have invented the Internet.*

Exercise: A *Ten* Question Quiz!

Supply the appropriate word for each blank, one that suits the description.

1. When your dog holds stubbornly to a stick, his refusing to let go indicates he is _____.

2. An officer who stands temporarily in control is a(n) _____.

3. Clem held a(n) _____ position on weed control, one that most of the landscape architects considered unreasonable.

4. To many of the customers, the showy display of jewelry stretched out on elegant lace tablecloths seemed tawdry and _____.

5. In a medical diagnosis, a bulging, twisted, or distorted vein or artery is considered to be a _____ blood vessel.

6. Someone who is troublesome, always looks for a fight, and thrives on arguments is _____.

7. Professor Kloochman, whose position at Evergreen State College has been guaranteed by the administration, is said to have _____.

8. Someone who is pompous, showy, or pretends to be superior is _____.

ANSWERS: 1. tenacious, 2. lieutenant, 3. untenable, 4. ostentatious, 5. distended, 6. contentious, 7. tenure, 8. pretentious

Ten Adjectives to Describe Animals

If you've read _Animal Farm_ in school or seen the movie _Babe,_ you may believe that animals have identifiable characteristics—some would say "personalities." At least the English language agrees, as it includes several adjectives that describe not only animals, but often humans as well.

What public figures—politicians, actors, newsmakers—might you describe with "animal" adjectives? For instance, Peter Lorre, the old-time character actor, who appeared in _Casablanca_ with Ingrid Bergman, had small _murine_ eyes and a nervous ratlike appearance. Actor Gary Busey has a long face and extra-large teeth, giving him an _equine,_ horselike appearance. As you scan the list, I'll bet you can think of other famous people (Sean Connery, Mel Gibson, Tiger Woods, Jack Nicklaus, and Dustin Hoffman) whose appearance suggests the adjectives below.

- **asinine** (relating to ass, donkey): *"That was a foolish, <u>asinine</u> comment, Chuck! You made yourself look like a donkey."*

- **bovine** (relating to cows, cattle): *The herd of women wandered through the farmers' market with a <u>bovine</u> purposelessness, randomly sampling fruits and breads from the streetside vendors.*

- **cetacean** (relating to whales): *At the <u>cetacean</u> exhibit, the schoolchildren saw videotapes of whales playing in Monterey Bay.*

- **equine** (relating to horses): *Among the many faces in the crowd, Phyllis noticed one man with a long, thin face, an <u>equine</u> appearance that reminded her of the horse she owned as a child.*

- **feline** (relating to cats): *In women's gymnastics, a <u>feline</u> grace, quickness, and balance are essential to success, at least at the Olympic level.*

- **lupine** (relating to wolves): *The <u>lupine</u> craftiness of Jack Nicholson in* Wolf *makes him both a dangerous and fascinating character.*

- **murine** (relating to rats): *When the mug shots were posted, Inspector Krumkieck observed that the criminal's tiny <u>murine</u> eyes were bloodshot and mean-looking, just like the rat in the horror film he had seen the previous night.*

- **ovine** (relating to sheep): *There was a kind <u>ovine</u>, sheeplike quality to MacDennis, who followed senseless orders without ever asking "Why?"*

- **porcine** (relating to pigs): _Actor Wayne Knight's <u>porcine</u> features have lent themselves well to comic roles, where he has used his chunky physique to advantage in sitcoms such as_ Third Rock from the Sun _and_ Seinfeld.

- **simian** (relating to monkeys, primates): _Al's long arms and <u>simian</u>, round-shouldered appearance shocked Marci, the next-door neighbor, who was afraid of monkeys._

Quiz: Match Game

For each adjective, identify the correct animal.

1. ovine		a.	pig
2. simian		b.	monkey, primate
3. lupine		c.	cat
4. murine		d.	wolf
5. feline		e.	rat
6. porcine		f.	donkey
7. cetacean		g.	cow
8. equine		h.	whale
9. asinine		i.	horse
10. bovine		j.	sheep

ANSWERS: 1. j, 2. b, 3. d, 4. e, 5. c, 6. a, 7. h, 8. i, 9. f, 10. g

Key Terms for Fine Dining: Absolutely Delicious!

How about a wonderful dinner at a four-star restaurant, the new place with the river view, where they have linen tablecloths, crystal water goblets, and waiters with names like _Jacques_ or _Enrique_? Are you ready? Let's review some of the terms that help you avoid getting lost after the _maître d'_ seats you and places a menu in your hands.

- **à la grecque:** cooked in the Greek style, with olive oil, herbs, lemon juice, and/or vinegar
- **à la nordmande:** in the Norman French style, cooked with cream and cider
- **béarnaise:** rich sauce of eggs, butter, shallots, herbs, and wine
- **blanched:** boiled briefly
- **coquille Saint Jacques:** scallops in the shell, prepared with special sauces
- **crimp:** to score meat for tenderizing
- **en brochette:** the French version of shish kebab— pieces of meat broiled on a skewer, often with vegetables
- **entrée:** the main dish
- **flambé:** covered with flaming brandy or cognac
- **fricassee:** veal or chicken cooked in a light sauce or gravy
- **hollandaise:** a sauce made with butter, egg yolk, lemon—the *coup de grâce* for eggs Benedict
- **jardiniere:** covered with a garnish of select vegetables
- **julienne:** a thin-sliced garnish of vegetable strips, delicately cooked
- **lyonnaise:** cooked or prepared with onions, especially potatoes, in the style of Lyons, a city in the east of France near the Rhône River
- **marinade:** fish, poultry, beef, or pork tenderized in a mixture of herbs, spices, oils, vinegars, or sauces
- **medallion:** a round, medallion-shaped cut of meat, usually the most tender cut

- **niçoise:** covered with onions, garlic, tomatoes, black olives, and other delights
- **paella:** a seasoned dish with fish, shellfish, vegetables, and rice—a specialty of the Spanish Riviera
- **parmentier:** garnished with or cooked with potatoes
- **pesto:** an Italian blend of basil, pine nuts, garlic, and olive oil
- **provençale:** the food traditions of southeast France, the Mediterranean region including coastal cities such as Nice and Marseilles; dishes are prepared with tomatoes and garlic
- **puree:** to blend or process vegetables or fruits to a fine pulp
- **satay:** spicy Indonesian sauce featuring coconut and peanuts
- **sauté:** to fry lightly in butter
- **sommelier:** a wine steward in a restaurant
- **vinaigrette:** a salad dressing or marinade made with oil, seasonings, and vinegar

Pop Quiz: A Culinary Review

Well, that was fun. Let's see what words you've added to your word bank. Match the food-related term below with its proper definition.

1. niçoise
2. crimp
3. coquille Saint Jacques
4. medallion

a. the wine steward
b. lightly fry in butter
c. a dressing or marinade of oil, seasonings, vinegar
d. a round cut of meat, usually a choice piece

5. puree	e.	veal or chicken cooked in light sauce or gravy
6. en brochette	f.	chunks of meat broiled on a skewer
7. vinaigrette	g.	boiled briefly
8. satay	h.	to blend or process vegetables or fruits
9. sautéed	i.	a rich sauce made with eggs, butter, shallots, herbs, wine
10. pesto	j.	spicy Indonesian sauce featuring coconut and peanuts
11. blanched	k.	covered with flaming liquors
12. fricassee	l.	garnished with select vegetables
13. paella	m.	cooked with onions, garlic, tomatoes, black olives
14. parmentier	n.	to score meat for tenderizing
15. béarnaise	o.	cooked with tomatoes and garlic, Mediterranean style
16. sommelier	p.	scallops prepared in the shells
17. flambé	q.	the main dish
18. jardiniere	r.	garnished with or cooked with potatoes
19. provençale	s.	an Italian blend of basil, pine nuts, garlic, and olive oil
20. entrée	t.	a Spanish favorite cooked with rice, fish, and vegetables

ANSWERS: 1. m, 2. n, 3. p, 4. d, 5. h, 6. f, 7. c, 8. j, 9. b, 10. s, 11. g, 12. e, 13. t, 14. r, 15. i, 16. a, 17. k, 18. l, 19. o, 20. q

Lessons from Mom:
Knowledge Is Where You Find It

One day, my long-suffering dad came home only to be told, "We've got to move!" Mom, it seemed, had read all the decent books in our branch library, and she was ready to resettle across town, where the university district branch had a different (and better) selection. The debate lasted several weeks, but I noticed during that time that Mom spent her spare moments packing items in boxes.

Mom transported books back and forth from the university district branch in rain, sleet, snow, and fog. She had a little two-wheeled metal cart that could hold two dozen hefty tomes, and sometimes the rack was full. But Mom took lots of detours along the way, at least when I was in tow. She was always stopping in stores and shops, big brick buildings and small three-walled kiosks, picking up pamphlets and magazines, riffling through flyers and newspapers. Sometimes it took two hours for us to walk the short distance home. When we arrived at the front steps, the little cart was usually groaning under the added load of papers that Mom had piled atop the books.

There was a lesson here, and she made it plain. "Knowledge is where you find it," she said. On those library trips, I learned what she meant. The library is a wonderful place to find new ideas, information, and words. But it is hardly the *only* worthwhile repository. The whole world is a library—and a good one—for those who know how to browse. Be on the lookout for places where you might learn new words: the library, a restaurant, a bus stop, a bulletin board. You name it.

Top Ten List: Great Places to Look for New Words

Here are some great resources I discovered while following Mom. If you want to find new words—and to hear them used in a variety of contexts—consider some unlikely stops along life's paths.

1. **The library.** And not just the stacks. Look around. A good library has computers with Internet access, government documents, and rows and rows of reference shelves. You can also find CDs, films, and novels on tape. Some of my favorites are the big volumes in the older but still compelling *Reader's Digest* series on language.

2. **Your kids' schools.** Visit the kids. Make arrangements with the teachers and staff. Then go down to their school and see what Jennifer and Hector are doing. The walls will be festooned with posters, maps, stories, announcements, pictorial displays, and daily assignments. You can visit the computer center, drop by the library, hang out at the writing center, and say *Hola!* at the Language Lab. Kids love new words. They're fascinated by language. You'll learn something, too.

3. **Used bookstores.** Mom always stopped there. If you want to surround yourself with a rich resource library—but don't want to pay superstore prices—head down Main Street and see what's lurking behind those display windows.

4. **The grocery store.** The grocery store has racks of newspapers and magazines—even some books to browse. I usually plop a copy of the local newspaper or *Atlantic Monthly* in my shopping cart, and while I'm waiting in line, I turn the pages. More often than not, I

find an article or two that makes me want to take the paper or magazine home.

5. **Temple, church, or mosque.** Did you know places of worship are open most days of the week? That's right— not just on the Sabbath or holy days. Inside, especially when you have a free moment, you'll find an amazing collection of books, papers, pamphlets, displays, and references. Many of these places of worship have reading rooms open to the public.

6. **The local college.** Take advantage. Even if you're not enrolled, you can usually go to the library, read the school newspaper, or wander through the student union. It's difficult to imagine a richer source for words.

7. **The video store.** Mom spent hours reading the blurbs and going through Roger Ebert's movie yearbook at the nearby video store. Those stops, of course, gave me the idea for the section on movie titles in Day 1.

8. **The workplace.** If you have computer access, just type in "Words" or "Word Play" on a search engine. Also, keep in mind that bulletin boards, annual reports, and e-mails are rich sources of new terms.

9. **Public buildings.** At the midpoint on our library path was a huge granite government building with offices for every bureaucracy from the Social Security Administration to the FBI. Mom was always stopping to order free booklets, pamphlets, and how-to manuals. The United States government publishes material on virtually every topic under the sun—not to mention outer space.

10. **The coffee shop.** Leave a little early in the morning and stop by your favorite street-corner latte shop. You'll find a cornucopia of reading material.

Tip of the Day

English is the most flexible, powerful, and productive language on earth, consisting of nearly half a million words, far more than any other language. Why? Among other things, English, once an obscure Germanic dialect, benefited from a series of historic encounters with other languages, sponging up new words from French, Old Norse, Latin, Greek, and scores of other languages.

If you carefully review the words in this book, you'll recognize the remarkable contributions of ancient and modern languages. Spending time unraveling the sources of English vocabulary words is a strong foundation for building your word bank.

When your grandparents or great-grandparents went to school, Latin and Greek were essential parts of the curriculum. For better or worse, the ancient languages have virtually disappeared from the public education curriculum in America, at least in terms of mandatory curriculum. Nevertheless, these languages remain central to your understanding of English.

I cannot underscore enough the importance of being aware of language history. Roots and prefixes like *pro-* and *-in* and *-ten* are the keys to further vocabulary development. In order to be a good word sleuth, you must cast an eye to those ancient cultures that left their marks on our language.

Words are important. A good vocabulary is a valuable resource. In ways too numerous to describe, a powerful lexicon opens doors and commands respect. Without doubt, good speaking and writing is a key to success and happiness.

Now that you have expanded your word bank and learned new skills in vocabulary, don't let your efforts lapse. Education is a lifelong process. Ten days is just a start. If you continue to read, write, and listen, your vocabulary will grow, along with your self-confidence and personal satisfaction. And remember—to gain the most from this regimen, you must practice. Today offers some great opportunities. Before turning out the light tonight, try to use *puckish, germane,* and *quid pro quo.* You'll go to sleep with a smile.

About the Authors

The Princeton Language Institute, based in Princeton, New Jersey, is a consortium of language experts, linguists, lexicographers, writers, teachers, and businesspeople that develops easy-to-read self-help books in a nonacademic format for writers, businesspeople, and virtually anyone who wants to enhance his or her communication and language skills. It is the creator of the *21st Century Dictionary of Quotations, 21st Century Grammar Handbook,* and *Roget's 21st Century Thesaurus,* with over one million copies sold.

Tom Nash, Ph.D., is a linguistics professor at Southern Oregon University. He is also a lecturer for the Oregon Council for the Humanities and a member of the Editorial Board of the *Oregon Literature Series.* Professor Nash, who has won study grants at Princeton, Yale, and the University of California–Berkeley, has been named Distinguished Professor for the Churchill Honors Program. He is the author of two other books, including *The Well-Traveled Casket: Oregon Folklore* (with Twilo Scofield). Nash lives in Ashland, Oregon, with his son Paul, a promising musician, and two old-maid cats.

The Philip Lief Group is a book developer based in Princeton, New Jersey, that produces a wide range of language and usage guides including *Grammar 101* and *Guide to Pronunciation.* The Philip Lief Group has been singled out by the *New York Times* for its "consistent bestsellers" and by *Time* magazine for being "bottom-line think tankers."